MILLIONAIRE LEGACY

Praise for
MILLIONAIRE LEGACY™

"Real champions don't stay down… They figure out another way… In this book, Thomas P. Curran features top performers who were able to achieve the highest level of success because they kept persisting and didn't give up. With an easy-to-follow blueprint, Thomas details their recipe for being successful."

—**Joe Theismann**
Former World Champion Quarterback for Washington Redskins
Motivational Speaker
www.joetheismann.com

"This power-packed book is loaded with valuable insights and ideas that will help you to achieve all of your financial goals."

—**Brian Tracy, Author**
The Way to Wealth
www.briantracy.com

"If you want to accelerate your progress forward, you definitely need to read this book and incorporate the eight millionaire success strategies into your life. This book gives you the opportunity of learning directly from Brendon Burchard, Bob Proctor, Mark Victor Hansen, James Malinchak, Sean D. Tucker, Steve Harrison, Russell Brunson, and Mike Filsaime. These highly respected experts share their proven blueprint for reaching ultimate victory."

—**Rick Frishman**
Best Selling Author, Publisher and Speaker
www.rickfrishman.com

MILLIONAIRE
LEGACY

8 MILLIONAIRE SUCCESS STRATEGIES
for Achieving Financial and Emotional Wealth

THOMAS P. CURRAN

CONTRIBUTING ADVISOR: Mike Filsaime

New York

MILLIONAIRE LEGACY
8 MILLIONAIRE SUCCESS STRATEGIES
for Achieving Financial and Emotional Wealth

© 2016 THOMAS P. CURRAN.

Published in New York, New York, by Morgan James Publishing. Morgan James and The Entrepreneurial Publisher are trademarks of Morgan James, LLC.
www.MorganJamesPublishing.com

The Morgan James Speakers Group can bring authors to your live event. For more information or to book an event visit The Morgan James Speakers Group at
www.TheMorganJamesSpeakersGroup.com.

Disclaimer: No warranties or guarantees are expressed or implied by the author, publisher, nor individuals featured within this book. This book is presented solely for educational purposes. None of the information shared with you is intended, nor should it be construed, to be professional, medical, psychological, financial, or legal advice. If you need help or assistance in any of these areas, consult a certified professional. Neither the author, publisher, nor anyone included within this book shall be liable for any physical, psychological, emotional, financial, or commercial damages, including, but not limited to, special, incidental, consequential or other damages. You are responsible for your own decisions, actions, and results. Any financial numbers referenced throughout this book and within "The Road to a Million Dollars: 10 Areas for Wealth Creation" section are simply estimates or projections, and should not be considered exact, actual or as a promise of potential earnings. All numbers are illustrative only. Being completely honest, there is no magic button for success. There is NO guarantee of making any money. This is determined by your motivation, knowledge, and willingness to take action. Your results, either positive or negative, are based solely upon your own actions and the decisions that you make.

The fact that an organization or website is referred to in this work as a citation and or a potential source of further information does not mean the author or the publisher endorses the information the organization or website may provide or the recommendations it may make. Further, readers should be aware that internet websites listed in this work may have changed or disappeared after this work was written.

The Millionaire Legacy™ Mindset Assessment, Scoring Chart, Assessment Report, and Evaluation of Results may NOT be copied, published, or duplicated in any manner without the consent of the author. Copies of this assessment may be purchased for your company, organization, or school upon request from the author. Please visit MillionaireLegacy.com.

A **free** eBook edition is available
with the purchase of this print book.

ISBN 978-1-63047-669-4 paperback
ISBN 978-1-63047-670-0 eBook
ISBN 978-1-63047-671-7 hardcover
Library of Congress Control Number:
2015908196

CLEARLY PRINT YOUR NAME ABOVE IN UPPER CASE

Instructions to claim your free eBook edition:
1. Download the Shelfie app for Android or iOS
2. Write your name in **UPPER CASE** above
3. Use the Shelfie app to submit a photo
4. Download your eBook to any device

Cover Design by:
Thomas P. Curran

Cover Image:
Sean D. Tucker flying the Oracle Challenger III

Cover Image Courtesy of:
Oracle, www.oracle.com

Interior Design by:
Bonnie Bushman
The Whole Caboodle Graphic Design

In an effort to support local communities and raise awareness and funds, Morgan James Publishing donates a percentage of all book sales for the life of each book to Habitat for Humanity Peninsula and Greater Williamsburg.

Get involved today, visit
www.MorganJamesBuilds.com

Habitat for Humanity®
Peninsula and
Greater Williamsburg
Building Partner

I am very thankful for the love, support, and
encouragement of a very special and beautiful friend,
Jenny, who touches me deeply within my heart and soul.

Our friendship is a wonderful gift that I treasure.
Jenny, I am truly blessed to call you my Best Friend
and for having you in my life.

Gratitude to Mike Filsaime for his Contribution to the Book

The author would like to give special recognition to Mike Filsaime whose contribution to this book was tremendous. This book would not have been possible without Mike's guidance and support.

To learn more about Mike Filsaime, please visit:
http://mikefilsaime.com

THANK YOU

The author would like to personally extend his deepest gratitude to the eight millionaires who agreed to be interviewed for this book. Without their participation, honesty, and receptiveness to share incredible information, this book would not be possible.

Bob Proctor
Brendon Burchard
Mark Victor Hansen
Sean D. Tucker
James Malinchak
Russell Brunson
Steve Harrison
Mike Filsaime

The author would also like to thank the following two amazing individuals who were interviewed for "The Heart of a Millionaire Chapter." Their willingness and kindness in sharing their stories are truly appreciated.

Captain Julie Clark
Karolyn Grimes

There is a special thank you for Captain Chesley "Sully" Sullenberger who was responsible for landing US Airways flight #1549 on the Hudson River when both engines were lost after a bird strike. Special permission was received to spotlight Captain Sully in the book.

Request Author as Keynote Speaker, Consultant, or Coach

Thomas P. Curran can provide consulting, training, and can speak to your organization about the success strategies outlined in Millionaire Legacy™.

To request Thomas to speak at your next event or to receive coaching:

Please visit: www.thomaspcurran.com

Share the Millionaire Legacy™ Message

Discounted pricing available for bulk orders of the book and special discounts are provided for schools. Copies of the Millionaire Legacy™ Mindset Assessment, Scoring Chart, Assessment Report, and Evaluation of Results may be purchased for your company, organization, or school.

For more information or to receive additional training, please visit:

www.MillionaireLegacy.com

CONTENTS

INTRODUCTION

"We're programmed to think it's difficult to earn a lot of money. It is not. It is easy. If you think it's difficult, you're making it difficult. You've got to learn how to earn money... Spend your days doing what you love, that is very important. You can set up sources of income where you create passive income... The secret of becoming wealthy is to have multiple sources of income."

—Bob Proctor

By making the decision to purchase this book, you are making an investment in yourself and that should be commended. The desire to acquire and learn valuable information will propel you to a higher level of emotional, financial, and personal development. Your momentum forward has just begun and will generate great results if you are willing to take action and incorporate the eight millionaire success strategies into your life which are featured within this book. Surround yourself with a positive vibrational energy being confident that you will achieve whatever you want from life.

For all of the highly respected individuals who were interviewed for this book, there was one major requirement. They could not be born into wealth; they had to be self-made millionaires. With a strong willpower to persist through challenging times, this was the catalyst for propelling them toward reaching their personal and professional goals. Their prosperity was acquired through hard work, dedication, and perseverance.

Sometimes, there is a negative stereotype regarding anyone who is rich. When you mention that someone is a millionaire, some people begin to make judgments that are completely false. They make an assumption that anyone with a lot of money was born into wealth and had everything given to them. To the contrary, there are a large number of affluent individuals who had to strive hard in order to reach their success.

When you talk to any of the remarkable individuals that are included in this book, you will find an amazing group of people who care deeply for their customers, clients, and employees. All of them have a desire to help others and give back. They are involved in a number of charitable organizations that they feel passionate about and this resonates throughout their personalities. The generosity that they carry deep within their inner spirit and graciously spread to other people is amazing. In a large number of cases, this is done discretely without any media attention and the public is generally unaware of these beautiful acts of kindness.

When you give to others with a *"Pureness of Heart"* and genuine concern, a ripple effect of love is created and this energy will flow back to you from the universe. Understand that when kindness and love is shared with other people, the feeling of gratification can be tremendous.

In the following pages, you are being given private access to affluent individuals and thought leaders. Their well-guarded secrets for becoming successful will be revealed through an easy-to-follow formula which can be duplicated. You will become part of the inner circle of exceptional people who are able to breakthrough barriers and obstacles in order to reach their dreams and goals.

Allow yourself to absorb the immense knowledge from the upcoming chapters and discover how to master the tactics utilized by millionaires.

Start your journey with the following steps:

1. Clearly establish your goals.
2. Integrate the eight success strategies into your life which are featured in this book.
3. Have a rock solid commitment to reaching your goals.
4. Keep focused on your ultimate objectives of what you want to accomplish.
5. Write out your aspirations in a focused manner and they should be prominently positioned in a location where they can be seen on a daily basis.
6. Visualize your dreams as if you are living them now.
7. Take decisive action starting today.

Think about this for a moment. A prosperous individual is someone who is able to maintain a determined attitude while taking action. As a result, they are able to achieve victory. On the other hand, there are some people who go through life barely able to pay their bills living from paycheck to paycheck unable to reach any type of financial freedom. In the pages ahead, a detailed plan for becoming wealthy will be shared. However, a solid commitment to reaching your individual objectives is paramount even though challenges may be thrown into your path.

When you begin to study the mindset of millionaires, it becomes apparent that they are always striving for the best. For them, complacency is not an option and they don't believe in "giving up." Surprisingly, after they reach the top of their profession, they are still pushing ahead to achieve other goals.

What prevents someone from reaching prosperity? Fear is a major component that stops most people from moving forward in their lives. This can be a fear of failure or even a fear of success. Sometimes, the unknown can be scary and people would rather stay stuck in their lives because they know what they currently have and it feels safe to them. However, this belief is a false sense of security and keeps a person trapped. At that point, there is no possibility of living life to the fullest potential. It is important to acknowledge that intellectual and emotional growth is a natural part of a healthy mind and spirit.

Sometimes, the "postponement strategy" is one method used in which excuses are made for not taking any action. With this type of attitude, the person believes that they will start their project at a later date and time. However, they never accomplish anything and continue to justify their inactivity through excuses.

Release Negative Scripts from Subconscious

Remove the anchors, weights, and scripts that are preventing you from reaching all of your goals. Throughout your life, you may have encountered people who said critical comments regarding your appearance, intelligence, talents, or ability to excel. Stop for a moment! Please realize that anyone who sent out this type of energy was coming from their own maladjustment and insecurities. In psychology, this is referred to as displacement. This is a concept where people will project their own negative feelings onto others. If we permit their criticism to penetrate our minds, then it becomes an integral part of our being. At that moment, any hope for feeling fulfilled and having self-confidence becomes deflated. For this reason, any type of detrimental statements must be discarded.

Realize that we all have an internal tape recorder deep within our subconscious mind which stores everything that we have been told in our life both good and bad. These messages can be from many years ago and reach back into our childhood. Subjectively, we make the decision to reject those statements or accept them as being the truth. Understand that negative comments from other people were recorded onto our internal tape recorder and stored deep within our subconscious library. These tapes have an automatic play button and will start playing on their own especially when challenging events are thrown into our path. As a result, we assume they are from our own thoughts or feelings. In reality, they are the words from other people that come up to our conscious level but they don't reflect our true being, identity, intelligence, or what we are capable of achieving. Whenever a negative thought comes into your mind, immediately erase and replace it with a positive affirmation about yourself. If you don't remove them, they will hold you down like an anchor thereby restricting any advancement forward.

Whatever has happened in your past is gone forever and this doesn't determine your self-worth or ability to succeed. Just as the highly respected professionals who are highlighted in this book, the ability to reach your dreams and goals is just a matter of making the decision to move ahead. Believe in yourself! You are capable of achieving whatever you want from life. If you can dream it, you can achieve it with determination, commitment, and perseverance.

Whether you believe in God or Jesus, it is time to release your past up to them or the universe. Appreciate the fact that your future destiny is not based upon your past; your ultimate happiness, joy, emotional well-being, and financial abundance is contingent upon the steps you start taking from this moment forward.

Mindset – Power of Positive Thinking

Have you heard of the "Law of Attraction?" With this concept, if you send out negative energy and thoughts to the world, you will receive back negativity. Likewise, if you send out positive thoughts, you will receive back positive energy.

If the mind becomes consumed with negativity, there is no room for positive ideas and feelings to flow openly. In other words, the power of thinking optimistically is a critical element that is needed to succeed. Despite the fact that there may be roadblocks and obstacles thrown into your path which must be overcome, the ability to maintain a confident attitude is vital.

For your ultimate victory, control your destiny through affirmative thoughts and feelings.

Step-by-Step Blueprint

You are going to learn the secrets of self-made millionaires and you will be given a step-by-step blueprint that will allow you to model after these respected leaders. Generally, this information is only known to a select group of affluent individuals that the majority of people will never have contact with. You now have access to these amazing individuals and their method for becoming prosperous will be clearly outlined.

Realize that your passion, motivation, and taking decisive action will be critical elements to your victory. Be open and receptive to learning the information contained within the following chapters.

Taking Action

When you begin to examine the real secret to success, you will find a common theme. Everyone who became a millionaire took ACTION! This is a key critical aspect that needs to be incorporated into your daily routine. This is called the "Magnetic Action Principle" and will be presented in Chapter 8.

The Magnetic Action Principle Formula is the golden key for achieving all of your dreams and goals in life:

Decisive & Consistent Action + Positive Vibrational Energy = Dreams & Goals

If you sit back and do nothing, you are making a conscious decision to stay exactly where you are in life. Even if you devote just one hour per day toward working on your goals and dreams, you will be surprised at your level within a few months.

Believe in yourself and realize that you have the power deep inside your heart and soul to accomplish all of your aspirations. The ability to attain financial and emotional freedom is waiting to be released. If self-doubt or limiting beliefs are allowed to control the mind, then moving forward will not occur and stagnation becomes prominent. It doesn't matter what negative comments other people may have told you. Continually remind yourself that you have the power within to achieve whatever you want from life.

As you read through the chapters in this book, realize that the millionaires shared their tactics in an easy step-by-step plan which can be duplicated. Allow yourself to be encouraged by their willpower to succeed thereby propelling your mindset to a higher consciousness of awareness. Learning the secrets of their mental process will create an excitement when you realize what you can accomplish. Wealth and optimal personal achievement are possible for anyone just by implementing a proven framework.

You can accomplish whatever you want from life. However, a person can have the best teacher, mentor, or coach in the world but if the success strategies aren't applied, nothing will happen. Time continues to pass by. You can make the choice to do nothing or you can make the decision to become an active participant on your life journey beginning now. Throw your excuses and procrastination out the window. Simply stated, the time for shaping your life in the direction that you want begins today!

Avoid regret by getting busy working on what you want to accomplish with a determined attitude of being triumphant. Within these pages, you hold the golden key and a proven blueprint to the life of your dreams. The impact of this plan can be powerful if you start moving forward. Commit yourself to finishing this book and implementing the eight success strategies which are used by millionaires on a daily basis.

The Millionaire Interviews

Interviews were conducted with the following millionaires for this book:

Bob Proctor
Author, Speaker, Consultant, Coach, and Mentor

Featured in the blockbuster hit, *The Secret*, Bob Proctor is widely regarded as one of the living masters and teachers of The Law of Attraction and has worked in the area of mind potential for over 40 years. He is the best-selling author of *You Were Born Rich*, and has transformed the lives of millions through his books, seminars, courses, and personal coaching. Proctor is a direct link to the modern science of success, stretching back to Andrew Carnegie, the great financier and philanthropist. Carnegie's secrets inspired and enthused Napoleon Hill, whose book, *Think and Grow Rich*, in turn inspired a whole genre of success philosophy books. Napoleon Hill, in turn, passed the baton on to Earl Nightingale who has since placed it in Bob Proctor's capable hands.

Brendon Burchard

Author, Motivational Speaker, and High Performance Trainer

Brendon Burchard is a #1 *New York Times* bestselling author. After surviving a car accident at the age of 19, Brendon received what he calls "life's golden ticket," a second chance. Inspired by his discovery that at the end of our lives we will ask, "Did I live? Did I love? Did I matter?" he turned his life around and quickly became a multimillionaire and legendary force in the motivational genre. He is one of the Top 100 Most Followed Public Figures on Facebook. His weekly YouTube show is the most viewed direct-to-camera personal development series in the history of YouTube. His motivational podcast, *The Charged Life*, debuted at #1 on iTunes across all categories in the United States and multiple countries.

Mark Victor Hansen

Co-Author of Chicken Soup for the Soul, Keynote Speaker, and Marketing Expert

Mark Victor Hansen is probably best known as the co-author for the *Chicken Soup for the Soul* book series and brand, setting world records in book sales, with over 500 million books sold. Mark also worked his way into a worldwide spotlight as a sought-after keynote speaker, and entrepreneurial marketing maven, creating a stream of successful people who have created massive success for themselves through Mark's unique teachings and wisdom. With his endearing charismatic style, Mark captures his audience's attention as well as their hearts. He assures people everywhere that "*with the right principles and mentors, you can easily create the life of your dreams.*"

Sean D. Tucker

Aerobatic Pilot and Chairman of EAA Young Eagles Program

Sean has been flying airshows worldwide since the mid-70's and has won numerous aerobatic competitions. In that time, he has flown more than 1,225 performances at nearly 500 airshows in front of more than 125 million fans. The level of professionalism and discipline in Sean's airshows is no coincidence. He practices his airshow routine three times every day. To endure the extreme physical demands of each routine, Sean maintains a rigorous physical training schedule, working out more than 340 days per year. Named as one of the Living Legends of Flight, Sean is a member of an elite group of aviators and astronauts that includes General Jimmy Doolittle, General "Chuck" Yeager, and John Glenn.

James Malinchak

Business and Motivational Speaker, Marketing Coach, and Speaker Coach

After growing up in a small Pennsylvania steel mill town near Pittsburgh as the son of a steelworker and a housewife, multi-millionaire James Malinchak is now one of most requested highest paid motivational and business speakers and business marketing coaches in America. Malinchak conducts live public seminars attended by new and beginning entrepreneurs, executives, celebrities, actors, professional athletes, professional speakers, and trainers. Malinchak also is called America's #1 speaker coach for anyone wanting to get started as a motivational speaker and start a personal achievement and corporate training company. Giving back is a big part of Malinchak's life and he has raised hundreds of thousands of dollars for various organizations and has donated thousands of dollars of his own money to help others.

Russell Brunson

Internet Marketing Training

Russell Brunson started his online business when he was a student and wrestler at Boise State University. His first product was a DVD teaching people how to build a potato launcher. He became fascinated with online marketing and tried every product and course he could get his hands on before coming up with his own system. With $20 and a simple idea, he sold more than a million dollars of his own products and services within a year of graduating. Russell's company, DotComSecrets.com, grew rapidly from a small one-man shop in his basement to a major online business with over 60 employees and more than $10 million in annual sales.

Steve Harrison

Publisher of Radio-TV Interview Report and Host of the National Publicity Summit

Steve Harrison's company helps authors, experts, and entrepreneurs refine, promote, and monetize their message. His company has helped launch such bestselling books as *Chicken Soup for the Soul, Rich Dad Poor Dad,* and *Men Are From Mars, Women Are From Venus.* According to Steve, "It's been really gratifying to help unknown authors become massively famous. When Jack Canfield and Mark Victor Hansen contacted us, their credit cards were maxed out, but they were committed to investing in their future and in doing as many interviews as possible. Today, almost everyone has heard of their *Chicken Soup for the Soul* book series which has sold over 500 million copies." He is also the co-creator of the *Best Seller Blueprint* with Jack Canfield.

Mike Filsaime
Internet Marketing Expert, Speaker, and Consultant
   Mike Filsaime was the General Manager of one of the nation's
largest auto dealers and he spent 14 years in the auto industry.
In 2004, it was time for Mike to leave the automobile sales
profession behind and seek out new opportunities that lie
ahead with the new frontier of Online Marketing. He decided
to work for himself and became a millionaire in just 3 years.
In January of 2006, he did his first million dollar product
launch. After that, his business grew from a spare bedroom to a
2500 square foot office and staff of 21 people. Mike started to
teach his methods, and from 2003-2009, Mike made a name
for himself as an Internet Marketing Expert. Between 2005-
2014, MikeFilsaime.com, Inc. and Mike Filsaime's other online
companies generated over 50 million dollars in revenue.

"The Heart of a Millionaire" Chapter
The following individuals are featured in "The Heart of a Millionaire"
chapter:

Captain Chesley B. "Sully" Sullenberger, III
Author, Speaker, Consultant, and Retired US Airways Captain
   Chesley B. "Sully" Sullenberger, III is best known for serving
as Captain during what has been dubbed the "Miracle on the
Hudson." After logging more than 20,000 hours of flight time,
Sullenberger became internationally renowned on January 15,
2009 when he and his crew safely guided US Airways Flight
1549 to an emergency water landing in New York City's frigid
Hudson River. The Airbus A320's two engines had lost thrust
following a bird strike. Since his retirement from US Airways,
Sullenberger served as co-chairman until 2013 of the EAA

Young Eagles, a program that inspires and educates youth about aviation.

Karolyn Grimes:

Actress and Unofficial Ambassador for the movie, "It's a Wonderful Life"
Karolyn is the actress who played ZuZu Bailey in the movie, *"It's a Wonderful Life"* with Jimmy Stewart. At the tender age of 4, Karolyn Grimes began memorizing lines and acting in the fantasy world of cinema. She worked with film legends John Wayne, Cary Grant, Bing Crosby, Loretta Young, Fred MacMurray, Betty Grable, and Danny Kaye. Her Hollywood career ended in her teens when her mother died from early-onset Alzheimer's disease and her father was killed in an automobile accident. She eventually married but that marriage ended in divorce. Then, she married again and her son committed suicide at age 18. Karolyn describes this time in her life as the most devastating. As she climbed out of that despair, her husband of 25 years died from lung cancer.

Captain Julie Clark:

Aerobatic Pilot and Retired Northwest Airlines Captain
Julie Clark is a pilot for more than 42 years and a retired Northwest Airlines Captain. She has logged more than 32,000 accident-free hours and she is also a highly respected aerobatic pilot within the aviation community. Julie Clark's air show routine takes her restored T-34, "Free Spirit," to the limits of its operating capability. In March of 2002, Julie received perhaps her highest honor with induction into the Women in Aviation Pioneer Hall of Fame of Women in Aviation, International. Julie is one of the few air show greats to be featured in a biography; her amazing story is told in *Nothing Stood in Her Way*.

Complete biographies and website addresses can be found at the back of the book.

Outline of Book

The eight success strategies used by millionaires for acquiring an abundance of financial and emotional wealth will be outlined within the first eight chapters. They include the following:

Chapter 1: Develop a Business Plan and Clearly Defined Personal Goals

Chapter 2: Overcoming Fear

Chapter 3: Failure is an Option

Chapter 4: Importance of Having a Mentor or Coach

Chapter 5: Having Persistence and Pushing Forward

Chapter 6: Mindset for Success

Chapter 7: Generosity and Gratitude

Chapter 8: Taking Decisive Action: Magnetic Action Principle (MAP)

In Chapter 9, "Key Elements for Employee Motivation", the secrets for becoming a highly effective and inspirational leader to your employees will be revealed. The ability to foster a dynamic and interactive relationship with your team members while inspiring them is a critical aspect to the success of your business. It will become apparent that employees can take on a different role within your organization and this can be the catalyst for developing a strategic alliance that will have a major impact to your business growth and profits.

As you move into Chapter 10, "The Heart of a Millionaire", the focus will be on three people including Captain Chesley B. "Sully"

Sullenberger, Karolyn Grimes, and Captain Julie Clark. They are being highlighted for their strong will to persevere through adversities. Allow yourself to be inspired by their dedication and willingness to push forward through many hardships in order to reach their ultimate objectives.

In Chapter 11, "Breakthrough to Financial and Emotional Wealth", the attention is centered on the major breakthrough that each millionaire experienced which propelled them to a higher level of achievement. Then, in Chapter 12, "The Millionaire Legacy", the focus will be on the legacies of each featured millionaire.

At the back of the book, there are three bonuses which include the following:

Bonus #1: *The Road to a Million Dollars: 10 Areas for Wealth Creation*
This section will outline ten areas for making money. In each area presented, you will be shown how to make $100,000. If you add them up, they equal one million dollars. There is no way to guarantee your success but if you actively apply the tactics presented throughout this book, there is a greater chance of becoming victorious. Ultimately, your results are based solely upon your own actions and the decisions that you decide to make.

Bonus #2: *Millionaire Mindset Assessment*
You can take this twenty-five question assessment in order to determine how closely your thought process is aligned with the mindset of a millionaire. After you complete the assessment, there is an evaluation provided so that you can understand your results. In addition, you will be provided with action steps that you can incorporate into your life that will allow you to model after the prosperous individuals featured in this book.

Bonus #3: *Mind Maps*
There are Mind Maps provided which clearly outline the eight millionaire success strategies and the key elements for employee motivation.

Accept the fact that your talents and gifts need to be shared with others. The exceptional individuals who were interviewed for this book share their knowledge and expertise with their customers through their products, coaching, courses, and seminars. You are going to discover their secrets for becoming wealthy but understand that taking action is at the top of the list for becoming triumphant.

Get emotionally involved in working toward your aspirations and let this resonate throughout your entire mind and body as you push forward with a determined attitude. Start taking the steps to reach your personal and business objectives! The time for ACTION is NOW!

"There is a difference between WISHING for a thing and being READY to receive it. No one is ready for a thing, until he believes he can acquire it. The state of mind must be BELIEF, not mere hope or wish. Open-mindness is essential for belief. closed minds do not inspire faith, courage, and belief."

—Napolean Hill,
Think and Grow Rich

4 Critical Elements to Achieving Success

(1) Generosity toward Others

Donate your time, knowledge, and money to other people with a genuine pureness of heart and have no expectation of receiving anything back in return. In addition, engage in "Three Small Acts of Kindness" in which you do something special for three people.

(2) Have Gratitude and be Thankful

Have gratitude and be thankful on a daily basis for what you currently have in your life and for what you will receive in the future.

(3) Maintain a Positive Vibrational Energy

On a continuous basis, send out a positive vibrational energy to the universe and allow this feeling to permeate throughout your mind, body, and spirit.

(4) Take Decisive Action on a Consistent Basis

Be open and receptive to taking decisive action on a consistent basis in order to achieve any dream or goal that you have in life.

Chapter 1

DEVELOP A BUSINESS PLAN AND CLEARLY DEFINED PERSONAL GOALS

"My business plan has two parts: 1. Get and keep customers. 2. Keep more money in my pocket than going out. That's how you get financially free. It's not about wealth; it's about financial freedom. You don't need a forty page business plan. You need to correctly position yourself the right way."

—James Malinchak

I n this chapter, the focus will be on the first success strategy utilized by millionaires. Before you can move forward, it is imperative to develop a business plan and clearly define the personal goals that you want to achieve.

Start with the following:

1

1. Write down the goals, dreams, and objectives you want to attain.
2. Make a list of the steps that you must take in order to reach your aspirations.
3. Take action while maintaining a positive attitude of being successful.

Without a clear plan of action, you will not achieve your ambitions.

In the book, *Think and Grow Rich*, Napolean Hill wrote, "Millions of men go through life in misery and poverty, because they lack a sound plan through which to accumulate a fortune. Henry Ford accumulated a fortune, not because of his superior mind, but because he adopted and followed a plan which proved to be sound."

For the most highly profitable companies, having a clearly defined business plan is vital. However, the ability to be flexible and willing to change your roadmap when there is a transition in the market or with your customers can determine the ultimate success or failure of your business. Allowing yourself to become rigid and unwilling to adjust your blueprint will have detrimental consequences for your revenue and profits.

Some executives and business owners will develop elaborate marketing plans that go on for pages and pages but they usually find their way into the bottom drawer of a desk that no one looks at after it is developed. You can have the most intricate and highly structured framework but if it doesn't apply to the real world, it is useless and can even result in the failure of your company. There are countless companies that had a great financial strategy on paper but they are no longer in operation.

According to James Malinchak, it is simply a matter of cutting costs and increasing margins without sacrificing value. "I believe we need to uniquely position you correctly in the right manner. We need to package everything to match that unique positioning and we need to figure out who your core ideal client is. Who do we partner with? If you're a financial planner, then you want to partner with estate planning attorneys because they already have your type of clientele and vice versa. If you are a video store owner, you want to partner with a pizza shop across the parking lot because they already have your type of customer. Who has your clients or customers already? Let's go, get, and keep a whole bunch of them. Let's make sure our margins are correct and we have a lot of built in profit and we keep more coming in than going out. That's my business plan," stated Malinchak.

Implementing Malinchak's tactic of partnering with other entrepreneurs that have your ideal client can be called "complimentary marketing." In other words, you will be developing a mutually beneficial agreement with a similar business owner who can drive customers to you. In return, you will be referring customers to them. This is a great example of a win-win situation for each party.

In order to formulate an effective business model, you should begin by developing a detailed list in the form of a mind map. This provides a graphical representation in an outline or flow chart diagram. This method allows you to organize the steps for reaching your goals. There are numerous mind mapping software programs which are available and can be found online by conducting an internet search.

Your mind map should be focused on the most important elements that you need in order to be successful. James Malinchak stated, "You don't need a forty page business plan." It should be concise and centered on the key points. You should be concerned about the following:

1. Provide high quality products, services, and programs which solve a problem.
2. Exceed the expectations of your clients.
3. Keep your current customers happy and welcome their suggestions.

4. Actively pursue new prospects.
5. Minimize the amount of lost revenue.
6. Generate profits on a consistent basis.

Although some people become very elaborate when developing a business plan, this is not required or even suggested. You don't need a marketing plan that is overwhelming and difficult to implement. Keep the focus on getting clients, keeping customers, and generating consistent profits.

Developing a framework for your business is a critical component for generating income. Equally important, having a blueprint for your personal life can give clarity and focus to the direction that you want to take individually. Your personal plan of action can have a great impact not only in regards to your life but also to your family and the people who are important to you. Spend some time clearly mapping out your goals. This can be accomplished by using a dream or vision board to post pictures of what you want to achieve.

In order to develop a dream board, any of the following items can be used:

- Bulletin board
- A poster
- Dry erase board
- A sheet of paper

On your board, post pictures and words related to what you want to attain within your personal life. For example, this may include pictures that represent the following: your dream house and vehicle, spending more time with family, taking vacations, and any other images that are related to living the life that you really want. Then the board should be placed in a prominent location where you can see it every day.

If you center all of your attention entirely on your business, you will be lacking within your personal life. It is healthy to have a balance in both areas. As a result, don't overlook your aspirations and spend quality time with your spouse, children, family, and friends.

Yearly Goals and Key Performance Indicators "KPI's"

A large number of entrepreneurs and top level executives will strategically detail a plan for one, three, and five years. In theory, this is a wise and a conservative approach to planning ahead but having flexibility and a willingness to change your blueprint is also crucial for the survival of your business.

In today's economy and with the advancement of technology, be receptive to altering your initial operational plan for your business because this is a critical factor for your ultimate victory. According to Russell Brunson, the ability to keep things fluid and liquid is necessary because everything is changing rapidly.

In order to determine if your organization is operating in an efficient manner, there needs to be a focus on the Key Performance Indicators (KPI's). The KPI's give a company an objective and unbiased way to compare the level of performance with their goals. KPI's can be uniform and standardized. However, if there are certain aspects not generally measured within your industry, you will have to devise your own set of KPI's that are unique to your business.

Some people get very detailed when considering KPI's and may want to examine every possible element. However, this may not be the best approach. Sometimes, it is better to keep things less complicated so it is easier to evaluate the overall results.

For example, when Brunson looks at the performance level of his membership site, he concentrates on the following:

- How many members are actively involved in the membership site every month?
- How many members have been added within a given month?
- How many members are lost within a month?

After examining these numbers, Brunson can devise a strategy for increasing low membership.

Critical Aspects for Business Success

1. Create a clearly defined business plan focused on acquiring customers and providing exceptional service that exceeds their expectations.
2. Understand what your competitors are offering so that you can go above and beyond them.
3. Ask your employees for their suggestions on how to improve products, services, and customer relations.
4. Utilize an education based marketing approach in which you share valuable information through free reports and audio / video training.
5. Encourage feedback from your clientele so that you can improve on your products and services. Post their positive testimonials on your website and use them in your marketing campaigns.
6. Actively utilize email and text messaging to keep in contact with your clients.
7. Use target specific advertising and the internet to spread the word regarding your company.
8. Develop an online presence including some of the following websites: YouTube, Facebook, Twitter, LinkedIn, etc.

How can a business ensure survival? The ability to stand above the competition and build trust is critical to acquiring and keeping clients.

We are experiencing a very challenging economic environment in which businesses are closing at an alarming rate. This can be scary for a lot of entrepreneurs who are in fear of losing their source of income. If you don't implement new marketing tactics, your company will not last through this turbulent economy. However, if you are receptive and open to gaining customers, you will generate substantial profits.

Employees – "The Great Asset"

Your employees can be a great asset in shaping your overall marketing plan and direction of your business. In a best case scenario, your team members are dealing directly with your clients and products. This gives them a unique insight into what is working and not working within your organization.

Share your business plan with your staff. They are crucial to increasing your revenue and profits. They need to know your objectives. Some entrepreneurs are secretive and will not release this information to anyone who works for them. As a result, this becomes detrimental to the operation of their company. Realize that your team members are there to support you.

Your employees can play a critical role in the development of your business goals. When you are devising your framework, the following aspects must be considered:

- Be open and receptive to reaching out to your employees for their suggestions on how to grow or expand your company.
- Talk to your staff and brainstorm with them.
- Respect your employees and their advice.
- Appreciate the significant impact that your team members have for your success.
- View your staff as an integral part of your business.

You might be surprised by their suggestions and ideas. They might give you a perspective that you never thought of before. Sometimes, it is possible to lose focus on key elements that can ensure victory. Input from your employees can be a valuable tool for the survival of your company.

In Chapter 9, we will focus on how to motivate and inspire your employees.

The Challenge

> *"I don't have a traditional business plan but every single morning I do some strategy work for my business. Everybody should spend ten percent of their working days focused on the bigger picture, on strategy. I'll take that strategy, work that first, figure out where I'm trying to go, how I'm going to differentiate, and how I'm going to add value. I'll break that down into projects, initiatives, and I'll start assigning teams and tasks. I have an end in mind, very clearly."*
>
> **—Brendon Burchard**

The ability to have definite goals and a written plan of action for your business and personal life is crucial for your ultimate victory. But the willingness to be adaptable and open to change can determine whether the results you achieve are negative or positive. Keep it simple and have a blueprint which is concise and to the point. If you become consumed with establishing an extremely detailed plan that is very long and complicated, you will be distracted from the most important elements of operating your business.

In order to reach your final destination, you need a roadmap. For any business to be successful, there needs to be a systematic approach to achieving desired objectives. Without a clearly defined strategy, the chances of prosperity are greatly minimized. With that point in mind, there needs to be careful thought and reflection when it comes to mapping out the direction of what you really want to achieve with your professional and personal goals.

Don't permit an over inflated ego to prevent you from being receptive to new and innovative ideas. In order to be competitive within your industry and acquire customers on a consistent basis, there needs to be flexibility with a focus on the future. If you had effective strategies in the past that generated great results, expand on them and make them better. Remember, you want to stand above your competitors and establish a positive and unique branding.

Your products and services should solve a problem. Also, customer satisfaction is critical for the survival of your business. Be willing to share some of your knowledge and expertise with your prospects and clients without any expectation of charging them. Yes, share some of your expertise for free. Let's face it. Your customers know that you need to make a profit but when you provide high quality information to them without always asking for money, a long-lasting positive impression will be implanted within their minds.

Millionaire System for Developing a Business Plan and Personal Goals

*1. Calculate expenses, revenue, profits, and
list the steps to achieve your personal goals.
2. Generate a strategy for acquiring
customers and keeping them.
3. Develop your business plan and begin a dream board.*

"We have written goals; we have a promotion schedule usually about three or four months out. We have goals for the year and we

list things when we're making decisions in terms of what's going to bring in the best ROI (Return on Investment) with the effort. How much time something's going to take? What's going to produce the most revenue and further the vision for the business? We have a written description for the business of what we're wanting to build."

—**Steve Harrison**

1. Calculate expenses, revenue, profits, and list the steps to achieve your personal goals

In order to devise an effective business plan, the following areas should be addressed:

- Projected Expenses
- Estimated Revenue
- Anticipated Profits

When you are calculating the above numbers, use a spreadsheet or computer program such as Excel to keep everything organized.

Sometimes, keeping things simple and to the point can be the key to customer acquisition and retention while generating revenue. Minimize expenses and generate more money in profits; this is the key component to your success.

When developing your company projections, closely examine how much you are spending in order to get a client. Be sure to average in your marketing costs. If you are paying more than the revenue generated from the customer, you have a major problem.

Furthermore, analyze your closing ratio. This allows you to examine the amount of people you have contact with compared to the number of people who actually buy your products and services.

For any personal goal that you want to attain, devote your time with the following:

- Commit yourself to doing your homework and research.
- Write out the dreams that you want to achieve.
- Make a step-by-step checklist of the action steps needed to reach your objectives.
- For each one of your action steps, put anticipated completion dates on a calendar.
- View your goals as if you already have them.
- Keep focused on positive thoughts.
- Take action NOW.

2. Generate a strategy for acquiring customers and keeping them

Customer acquisition is at the top of the list for the survival of any business. However, there are a number of entrepreneurs who are missing a very simple approach for increasing clients. They are not collecting email addresses from people who come into their business or visit their websites. But, for the entrepreneurs who do obtain this information, they generally don't have an effective marketing strategy to promote their products and services.

Think about this. How many stores or websites do you visit which never ask for your email? When someone comes into your business or stops at your web page, you have the opportunity to obtain a dedicated client. However, when a potential customer walks out the door or leaves your website, you have most likely lost them forever. Can you begin to realize how much money is being lost in revenue by not asking for someone's email? Obtaining emails and utilizing effective campaigns could determine your eventual success.

If you survey business owners, you will discover two major weaknesses: a large percentage of them are unwilling to give something of value away for free and they aren't collecting email addresses. When a person walks into your store or visits your website, give them something of high value in return for their email address. This is called reciprocity. Reassure them that you only want this information so you can send them your newsletter and "special discounts" for the "inner circle clients" on your list. Let them know that these exclusive discounts are just for members. Tell them that you respect their privacy and will not disclose any of their contact information with anyone else.

The "old way of doing business" will bankrupt your company. If you are rigid and unwilling to change an old mindset, the future success of your business is greatly diminished. From a psychological perspective, when you give something of great value away for free through a report or video, you elevate yourself to a higher level and establish your reputation for being a trusted expert. As a result, your prospect will be more likely to make a purchase from you.

Your email marketing campaign should not be constantly focused on selling a product or service. Be willing to share valuable information without always asking for money. This type of approach will establish your credibility. During your email campaign, offer a discount to everyone on your list for being a valued member of your "inner circle." In today's economy, an innovative approach must be utilized in order to ensure the victory of your company. Be willing to go above and beyond your competitors.

3. Develop your business plan and begin a dream board

Do your research and start developing your business plan. This framework for your business is an essential element for your success.

You must establish a strategy for what you want to accomplish and you need to list the steps that will get you there.

In reference to reaching your personal goals and dreams, the following steps are required:

- Write down your goals.
- Incorporate the daily habit of using positive affirmations.
  - An affirmation is a statement or phrase that you repeat on a consistent basis regarding the intention you want to receive.
- Create a dream board with all of your pictures prominently displayed.

After you post your dreams on a vision board and make your intentions known, you will begin to radiate a vibrational energy throughout your mind, spirit, and body. As a result, your enthusiasm and commitment to reaching your goals will become stronger. You will discover that your momentum forward is accelerated because you realize that your aspirations will become reality.

Lessons Learned

"You need a set plan of action… You have to know the destination so that you can create a roadmap to get there… In business, how are you prepared to navigate? You have to navigate without steering off course. If you don't plan; then you're planning to fail. So, it's very important for you to know the destination and plan properly for it."

—Mike Filsaime

It is important to understand that in today's new economy, you generate revenue and profits with a systematic approach that includes the following aspects:

1. Establish yourself as a trusted expert.
2. Share your valuable expertise for free with your clientele.
3. Educate your customers and show them how your products and services solve their problems.
4. Invite your prospects and clients to invest in your products.

The most successful entrepreneurs and executives have a clear vision of what they want to accomplish. They will utilize mind maps to outline the steps that need to be taken and then incorporate this into their marketing plan.

As referenced by James Malinchak, you should not be running your business as if it were a multi-billion dollar enterprise like an Apple or Starbuck's. If you are a small business owner, you don't want to be doing things the same way you would if your company was bringing in a billion dollars in revenue. "Nobody needs a brand, everybody needs a unique and right positioning… you need to be uniquely and correctly positioned," stated Malinchak.

Malinchak focuses on the following areas to ensure success:

1. Position yourself correctly in the right manner.
2. Package everything to match that unique positioning.
3. Figure out who your core ideal client is.
4. Determine who you will partner with who has your clients already.
5. Go, get, and keep a whole bunch of clients and customers.
6. Make sure margins are correct with a lot of built in profit.
7. Keep more money coming in than going out.

It is essential to focus on expenses, revenue, and profits. If this is not your area of expertise, then reach out to accountants and advisers who are familiar with your industry. The most important aspect for the survival of your company is the acquisition and retention of customers. Provide the utmost service to your clients that exceed their expectations. Ensure that you are addressing their concerns while solving their problems. Understand that your team members play a vital role in this process.

Become very active with your prospects and anyone who made a purchase from you in the past so that you can find out what they want. As an entrepreneur, one of the biggest secrets for your success is to understand the needs of the client. If you survey them and ask them exactly what they are looking for, you'll be able to direct your resources in that direction. If you are non-receptive to their needs, you might lose your business. Anyone who is stubborn and unwilling to work directly with their clients is setting himself or herself up for failure. In today's challenging economic environment, the customer's desires are the utmost importance. It is easy to forget this aspect and get lost in just running the business; don't allow yourself to fall into this trap.

Without a consistent stream of clients, a business will fail. Don't allow yourself to get stuck within your own idea of what you think the buyer wants. Ask them for their suggestions and their concerns should be respected.

Remember to keep your personal aspirations at the top of your list. It is imperative that you write them down and organize a dream board that can be placed in a location where you are able to see it every day. Focusing on your vision board enables you to send out a positive energy to the universe stating that you are open and receptive to receiving your goals. By writing your personal goals down, having a dream board, and taking action, you will put yourself on the right path to reach your ambitions. As a result, your desire to achieve your aspirations will begin to pulsate stronger and your motivation will increase significantly.

Master Mind Action Steps

Action Step #1: Get a spreadsheet or open an Excel document on your computer and calculate your expenses, revenue, and profits. Analyze the numbers and determine what areas need improvement. For your personal goals, make a list of your hopes and dreams. Write down as many of your aspirations that come to mind and number them as far as importance.

Action Step #2: Think of businesses that have the same clientele that you want. Contact them and offer them a barter deal where you will promote them to your customers if they promote you to their customers. If they aren't receptive to this idea, offer them a referral fee for any client they send to you who becomes one of your paid customers.

Action Step #3: Print out your business plan and share it with your team members. Ensure that the plan is posted, clearly visible, and available for all employees to review. For your personal goals and dreams, start a dream board that has pictures which represent your aspirations. This vision board should be posted where it can be seen on a daily basis.

> *"I have a definite goal for the business and I set it with my business partner. We work on a number of different projects. The whole company works on them all the time and we review them. We have company meetings on a regular basis. We review the objectives that we want to reach in each part of the company. We encourage everybody in the company to have their own personal goals that would be in harmony with the company goals."*
>
> **—Bob Proctor**

Chapter 2
OVERCOMING FEAR

"When you're going after what you want, you're going to experience fear because you're getting out of the box. You're getting out of your comfort zone. You're getting out of what you're use to doing; living, and that causes fear. I call that a terror barrier and you've got to go through the terror barrier. And the only way you can do that is to face the thing you fear."

—Bob Proctor

Throughout history, fear has stopped countless people from achieving ultimate success. When it arises to a conscious level, it has a tendency to paralyze a person and prevent them from making any advancement toward their dreams or goals. However, with a committed attitude and passion to achieve your aspirations, fear can be reduced or eliminated.

Almost everyone will experience fear and the level of intensity will vary from person to person. Some people can push through this sensation and not think twice about it. For other individuals, fear will prevent them from moving onward. Nevertheless, with a steadfast determination and implementation of effective coping mechanisms, the probability of becoming victorious is significantly increased.

"One can choose to go back toward safety or forward toward growth. Growth must be chosen again and again; fear must be overcome again and again," stated American psychologist Abraham Maslow. In order to grow emotionally, keep accelerating your momentum forward. If you make the decision to stay stuck at a certain point in life because of a false sense of security, the tremendous life that you could have will never emerge. When effective strategies are implemented, you will be able to handle any challenging issues thrown into your path.

Abraham Maslow became well-known for creating the "Hierarchy of Needs," a framework for describing human motivation. According to Maslow, there are five needs:

Need for Self-Actualization
Esteem Needs
Love Needs
Safety Needs
Physiological Needs
—**A. H. Maslow**
A Theory of Human Motivation

The highest level in this model is self-actualization. If this level is not fully satisfied by doing what we are meant to do, we will develop "discontent and restlessness." Maslow noted, "A musician must make music, an artist must paint, a poet must write, if he is to be ultimately happy. What a man can be, he must be. This need we may call self-actualization." In other words, the desire to achieve personal growth and live our dreams is the utmost importance. However, the major force keeping us from this achievement is our apprehension.

Three Sources of Fear

For most of us, fear generally comes from three sources:

1. Uncertainty over a brand new situation that was never experienced before.
2. A loss of power and belief you have no control.
3. Pre-programmed conditioning which is buried deep within the subconscious mind.

Sometimes, emotional distress can develop almost immediately. At the exact moment it begins, we make the decision to accept or reject this feeling. If we accept it, we will stop completely and not move ahead. But if we decide to reject it, we will push onward with a firm confidence.

You must recognize that you have total control over fear and it can only influence your life if you allow it that power. Make the decision to immediately release this emotion when it slides into your consciousness and don't permit it the chance to consume your mind. Whatever thoughts you conceive within your mind and hold onto at a conscious level can transform into an outward manifestation presenting either positive or negative consequences. Also, your thoughts can trigger physiological responses in your body. In order to avoid an unfavorable physical reaction, decrease or stop a fearful response to a given situation at the onset.

There are countless individuals with great talents you never heard of because they abandoned their dreams when confronted by a phobia. They had a message, skill, or gift to share with the world but they just gave up. Unfortunately, their valuable contributions to society are missing. In later years, they will most likely develop remorse because they walked away from their passion and never achieved their ultimate goal. Therefore, permit yourself to learn from their mistakes and keep striving to reach your objectives so that you never experience regret in later years.

Brendon Burchard wrote in the *Millionaire Messenger,* "You are here to make a difference in this world, and the best way to do that is to use your knowledge and experience (on any topic, in any industry) to help others succeed." Burchard and the other respected individuals highlighted within the pages of this book passionately share their expertise with their customers through their products, services, seminars, and coaching.

It has been said that "energy flows where attention goes." In other words, you will attract into your life whatever you focus on. If your mindset becomes pessimistic, your overall energy will radiate negativity. As a result, this mental state will prevent you from reaching your aspirations. But if you center your attention on being victorious through whatever incident is causing you anguish, you will be successful.

Everyone has experienced being fearful in the past and all of us will most likely experience it again in our future. When you become scared over a certain event, focus your attention on achieving a positive outcome. Over the years, you may have conditioned yourself to run away from any frightening events. The tendency of human nature is to seek out pleasure and avoid any type of pain. However, it is important to realize that you can immediately change this limited thinking. Allow yourself to look beyond the obstacle in your path and focus on your ultimate destination.

Fear is Temporary and NOT Permanent

When people become scared, there is a key point often overlooked. Know that whatever fearful situation you face is only temporary and not permanent. This concept is further illustrated by the story of Karolyn

Grimes, an actress who is featured in Chapter 10 of this book. Grimes starred in the 1946 holiday classic film, *It's a Wonderful Life*, with James Stewart and Donna Reed. However, she did not live a fairy tale life as shown in the movies. To the contrary, she faced many hardships but was able to overcome challenging times by realizing they were only brief setbacks and everything would eventually work out. Throughout it all, the ability to look beyond her current challenges and visualize a positive future was Karolyn's motivating force for pushing ahead. By implementing Karolyn's strategy, anyone can navigate through adversities having confidence that the struggle is only a momentary problem.

Uneasiness may arise from difficult situations because you are uncertain regarding the outcome of a particular event. But confidence will increase when you maintain a willingness to keep traveling down the road even when problems are encountered. Stay committed, believe in yourself, and take steps that will help to ensure your victory.

**Confidence + Determination + Action =
Positive Outcome & Results**

Fear can become distorted to the point where it develops into an intimidating barrier that appears unconquerable. If this happens, there is no way to progress after that point and stagnation becomes prominent. If you are interested in reaching emotional and financial prosperity, it is essential to minimize or remove the thoughts that hold you down.

Any emotion you feel is either enhanced or diminished by the amount of importance you attach to it. In other words, if you believe that fear can't be overcome, this thought will control your mind and you will become stuck. However, if you view fear as a minor setback that can be conquered, you will be able to reach your goals.

Consider this. If you obsess over whatever matter is causing distress, it will only expand bigger and bigger to a point where you will be unable to progress forward. In some cases, you might experience a physiological response where your heart is racing and perspiration is developing on your body. When this happens, your anxiety level rises very quickly. In a short time, you will become immobilized without any ability to take action. The key solution to this problem is to deescalate the incident before it reaches that point.

In psychology, the concept of classical conditioning was discovered by Ivan Pavlov. This theory describes how we condition ourselves to respond to particular situations in a certain manner. In order to prove that a fear response could be acquired in this manner, John B. Watson, the founder of behaviorism, along with his assistant, Rosalie Rayner, conducted an experiment with a young boy who was called "Little Albert." They exposed Little Albert to a white rat and conditioned him to be fearful every time that he saw the rat. As a result, they demonstrated that fear could be a learned response.

Over time, you may have taught yourself to become scared when certain incidents occurred in your life. When you are presented with similar circumstances, nervousness rises from your subconscious level to your conscious level. Then, fear may become dominant and you will find yourself unable to formulate an effective plan. It is essential to recognize that classical conditioning is a learned response and you can replace a negative association with a positive one. By reprogramming your reaction to a given event, you will change your thinking into a winning mentality.

Overcoming Fear with Sean D. Tucker and Captain Sully

When the subject of flying is discussed, some people become very scared and restless. The fear of flying has stopped many individuals from taking trips, visiting with family members, and going on vacation. However, when you analyze the huge number of commercial airline flights that take off and land safely on a daily basis, it becomes apparent that any apprehension regarding this matter is simply a personal feeling. Statistics prove that flying is one of the safest ways of traveling. Although some people allowed themselves to be consumed by a phobia, there are a large number of individuals who were able to conquer their fear of flying.

Let's take a look at Sean D. Tucker who is considered to be one of the best solo aerobatic pilots in the world. As a highly respected pilot within the aviation community, he has the ability to execute phenomenal aerobatic routines with exact precision.

Before Sean D. Tucker was able to achieve his reputation as an aerobatic pilot, he had a major challenge to overcome. Several years ago, he watched his friend die in a skydiving accident. After that, he developed a deep fear of flying and would panic at the controls of the airplane. At that point, Sean had a critical decision to make. He could walk away from his passion or he could embrace it directly. Sean decided to confront his fear head on and he took an aerobatic flight with Amelia Reid, a flight instructor and airshow performer at Reid-Hillview Airport in San Jose, California. When Amelia taught Sean how to safely perform maneuvers, he became an "aerobatic junkie." From that moment on, he was able to release all of his anxiety and his fear completely disappeared.

Tucker's dedication to pursue his dream was greater than any fear. Stop for a moment! If this worked for Sean, it can work for you. Realize that the majority of time our apprehension is blown out of proportion. When this happens, the first inclination is to run away and not look back. But, our perception at that point is not based in reality; we are simply controlled by anxiety. For this reason, maintain a realistic view of the fear you are facing and recognize that it can be discarded.

Tucker eloquently stated, "For the first time, I acknowledged a huge fear and fell so in love what I was afraid of… I am going to acknowledge every fear. I am going to live my dream because I found out what really made me empowered was my passion." Sean continued to pursue his dream with determination and a focused mindset. His vibrational energy was centered on his goal and he took decisive steps in order to be triumphant.

As the result of Sean's hard work, perseverance, and dedication, he has become a prominent aerobatic pilot within the aviation community. Sean has flown in numerous airshows across America including the Chicago Air and Water Show. He has flown more than 1,225 performances at nearly 500 airshows in front of more than 125 million fans. If you attend an airshow and look toward the sky, chances are pretty good that you will find him flying his red Oracle Challenger III biplane and performing his aerial routine referred to as *"Sky Dance."* In recognition of his great talent and professionalism, Sean is the only civilian performer ever to be allowed to fly in a close formation with both the Blue Angels and Thunderbirds.

Although he has reached excellence and perfection within his profession, Sean does not take his accomplishments for granted. He still practices his aerobatic routine three times a day even though he has performed it countless times. When you talk to Sean D. Tucker, you will find a grounded individual who is concerned about providing an excellent performance for the spectators who are in attendance at the airshows.

Sean D. Tucker's financial statement does not provide his inspiration. Sean's true motivational energy source is his concern for the spectators and his team members. Without a doubt, his passion for flying is deeper than any possible fear. While acknowledging that he has a dangerous profession, Sean D. Tucker continues to passionately live his dream on a daily basis.

In a later chapter, Captain Chesley "Sully" Sullenberger will be highlighted in detail. He was the captain of US Airways Flight 1549 which departed from LaGuardia Airport in New York on January

15, 2009. Just after takeoff, the plane struck a flock of birds and lost both engines. As a result, the plane lost forward thrust and Sully was forced to make a landing on the Hudson River. This challenging event would scare any of us but Sully did not allow this emotion to consume his mind. Instead, he focused on safely landing the plane and is recognized as a hero for saving 155 passengers and crew members.

Captain Sullenberger was literally thrown into a crisis situation that he never faced before but he was able to take appropriate steps to safely land the US Airways Airbus A320 on the Hudson River. The fact that he was able to push his fear to the side and put the safety of his passengers and crew members above himself is highly commendable.

How did Sean D. Tucker and Captain Sullenberger eliminate fear? The answer is simple… They did not become frozen in time by an unhealthy mental state; they continued onward with a rock solid confidence of being successful. Their positive momentum forward was so strong that success followed naturally.

The Challenge

"Fear can either be something you use to protect yourself and curl up, or it can be used as something to grow yourself and to stand up. It can be used as something that doesn't minimize you, but actually activates you."

—Brendon Burchard

Fear is one response that can stop anyone from reaching optimal performance and becoming financially secure. If you allow a phobia to have complete dominance over your life, it will prevent you from achieving any of your wishes. So, the challenge is to overcome your fear being confident that you will be victorious in the end. Make the decision to shape your own destiny and take that leap forward without getting stuck by any obstacles in your path. You have the ability to achieve happiness and financial prosperity.

When confronted by a terrifying situation, people want to turn and run away because they mistakenly feel a loss of power. In reality, having total command over your future is the ability and willingness to persevere through whatever life may throw at you. If you give up, any control that you did have magically disappears and your goals are crushed.

Will certain events elicit panic and stress? Of course! In psychology, there is a well-known concept referred to as "fight-or-flight" which was first noted by Walter Cannon. This simply means that when someone feels scared over a given event or situation, they will either stay and fight or run away. What do you want for your future? Are you willing to stay and overcome the hardships so that you can reach your dreams?

When you want to override a negative emotional response, make an immediate decision to release that sensation and center your thoughts on what you really want to accomplish. Continually remind yourself that whatever anxiety you are facing is only temporary and you will achieve your aspirations.

Millionaire System for Overcoming Fear

1. Don't focus on fear, minimize it.
2. Visualize the bigger picture; your goal.
3. Decide on a plan and take action.

"Fear comes from the unknown and what we choose to focus on. Worry is nothing more than the misuse of your mind. Start focusing on what if it does work versus what if it doesn't... Look at all the great things that could happen."

—**James Malinchak**

1. Don't focus on fear, minimize it

As you travel down the road of life, it is inevitable that you will be presented with roadblocks. When this happens, you may have feelings that will rise to your conscious level and that will scare you. At this point, minimize your mental perception of what is making you fearful and throw your anxiety out the window. There is no time to think about fear and over analyze what decisions you should make. Proceed forward with a determined attitude of getting beyond that obstacle in your path.

A further look at Captain Sully, who had to make split second decisions when his plane struck the flock of birds, illustrates an effective method of minimizing fear. The following is a passage from Captain Chesley "Sully" Sullenberger's book, *Highest Duty: My Search for What Really Matters*:

> *"Two thoughts went through my mind… This can't be happening. This doesn't happen to me. I was able to force myself to set those thoughts aside almost instantly… I knew that I had seconds to decide on a plan and minutes to execute it. I was aware of my body. I could feel an adrenaline rush. I'm sure that my blood pressure and pulse spiked. But I also knew I had to concentrate on the tasks at hand and not let the sensations in my body distract me."*

The above words from Captain Sully show that he had a normal psychological response to the situation that was literally thrown into his lap. His experience was so pronounced that his body exhibited signs of distress. Simultaneously, Sully made the conscious decision "to concentrate on the tasks at hand and not let the sensations in my body distract me." Doubt came in and he pushed it to the side instantly so that his concentration could be focused on safely landing the plane on the Hudson River.

According to James Malinchak, think back to all the things that you were nervous about in the past. After reflection, you'll come to appreciate the fact that you were able to bypass the frightening events and push in front of them. In addition, you come to discover that you weren't really fearful while overcoming those challenges. Now put yourself in that same state of mind and focus on "what if it does work versus what if it doesn't."

If you want to achieve the same level of success as the highlighted millionaires in this book, you need to control your feelings with a solid pledge that you are a winner and nothing will stop you. Most importantly, this should be your daily mental process. At times, you may get knocked down but just keep getting up and advancing toward your objectives. If an obstacle gets thrown into your path, either jump over it and keep going or find an innovative solution to get around it. Keep yourself open to being triumphant.

2. Visualize the bigger picture; your goal

Bob Proctor noted, "I think the right goal scares and excites you at the same time. It excites you because it's what you want. It scares you because it's not in harmony with your conditioning. So it sets up a fear vibration, but you must face it. You can't let the fear win. You face it and then the fear will leave you."

Some of the most successful millionaires were able to visualize their eventual goal and make this their motivating force on a daily basis. Mark Victor Hansen conquered the fear of rejection in order to get *Chicken Soup for the Soul* published. The book, co-authored with Jack Canfield, was rejected by over 140 publishers before a small publishing company agreed to publish the book. After this, *Chicken Soup for the Soul* was turned into a series and sold millions of books.

Many people are afraid of rejection and will turn away from it very quickly. They spend more time trying to avoid it instead of just moving through the rejection with a persistent attitude. Experienced sales professionals will tell you that the more "No's" they receive only bring them closer to getting a "Yes" from a potential client. When you recondition your mind to focus on the greater achievement, your entire attitude will change.

What is your goal? What are your aspirations? Become clearly focused on what you want and set yourself into an energetic vibrational state that will get you to your destination. As you incorporate this mindset, feel yourself living your dream just like it is happening now.

3. Decide on a plan and take action

Having a clearly defined plan for what you want to accomplish is critical for your success. It is important to write your plan down in a concise manner and be willing to take action steps every day. When you start, you may be limited on time so focus your attention on high-priority tasks and don't get lost surfing the internet, sending trivial text messages, or watching television. If you are willing to dedicate at least an hour or two a day to working on your dreams, you will be amazed at what can be accomplished within thirty or sixty days. It is matter of prioritizing your time so that you can reach your personal and business objectives.

If you center your attention on taking action, you will find that you don't have time to obsess over being anxious. Accept the fact that you can overcome any doubt that may arise from your subconscious level.

Lessons Learned

"Fear is a psychological feeling that is in our mind and it is not real. It is a state of mind; an internal event that has not yet happened. That's all it is. As human beings, fear is built into us and it is a mechanism to help us deal with danger. Even so, we can't let it get in our way and obscure our judgment because we will make

irrational decisions... We have to understand that without risk, there can be no reward... Realize that you have to evaluate the danger with a clear head, be objective, don't lie, and welcome risk into your business."

—Mike Filsaime

Giving into fear will stop you from reaching your dreams, goals, and financial wealth. At times, overcoming this challenge may seem like a major task but realize that your emotions are not necessarily based on reality. It has been said that "Feelings are not Facts." To clarify, understand that feelings are usually subjective and they are not based on any statistical facts.

As Bob Proctor discovered, you are going to experience fear because you are getting out of your comfort zone. He calls this the "terror barrier;" you have to go through the terror barrier by facing the thing you fear. Comprehend that you have the power and control to remove any fear which may emerge in your life.

From an intellectual perspective, it is imperative that you don't make life altering decisions based upon a feeling that may pop quickly into your head from a subconscious level. Any decision that you make at that moment is likely to be detrimental to your future. Furthermore, making impulsive choices could prevent you from attaining the great future you are meant to have. Contrary to what anyone may have told you, a phenomenal life is within your reach if you are open and receptive to taking action and applying the eight success strategies which are outlined in this book.

For Sean D. Tucker, his love for the spectators and passion for flying propels his mindset to a higher vibrational level. Likewise, when Captain Sully lost both engines on his plane, he did not focus on being scared. The safety of his passengers and crew were the utmost importance and he knew that he had to safely land the plane. As a result, Sully elevated himself to a higher intellectual level which allowed him to achieve a successful outcome.

When you become totally dedicated to reaching your final objective, there is no room for a negative state of mind to hold you back or stop you. Keep centered on your eventual goal or dream. With this firm attitude, even though there might be minor setbacks, nothing will prevent you from reaching the life that you want.

There may be several routes you can take to reach your dreams and goals but the ability to be flexible is critical. Permit yourself to get creative with possible alternatives. There might be an obstruction in the roadway but there are also several possible solutions for getting past it. Remember to look beyond your current state of mind and visualize a perfect ending that will make you very happy. Surprisingly, this may be the extra jolt that you need to get motivated.

If you are able to anticipate situations ahead of time that may cause apprehension, be proactive and brainstorm possible solutions. You will discover that your coping level for dealing with stressful events improves greatly. As this method of dealing with fear becomes a habit, you will be mentally prepared to handle any challenge with confidence.

We all have aspirations that we need to reach. You may have a great product, service, or message to share with the world that could help a lot of people. However, if you allow anxiety to prevent you from achieving what you are meant to do, your energy level will become deflated and you won't feel complete.

Live life completely by reaching all your dreams and goals! Become financially and emotionally secure. You have the power deep inside your heart and soul to achieve great potential. The millionaires interviewed for this book have proven it is possible to abolish fear and reach abundance.

It is important for you to honor and respect whatever your ambitions may be. As a result, don't allow any type of fear to hold you back from reaching your true passion in life. After reaching your goals, the great sense of accomplishment and self-worth that you feel will be phenomenal.

Mastermind Action Steps:

Action Step #1: Write out what you fear in very small letters on a piece of paper or dry erase board. Then throw out the paper or erase your fear from the board. This is one symbolic technique which can be used to completely abolish your fear. Realize that whatever event is causing you panic can be minimized and then discarded.

Action Step #2: Write down your goals on a piece of paper in big letters. Tape this paper to your refrigerator or door where you can see it every day. Visualize your dreams as if you are living them right now. Know that fearful events may arise but if you keep your mind focused on your aspirations, you can push through whatever is blocking your way.

Action Step #3: Write out your plan in a concise manner and start taking action. Keep your eventual goal as the ultimate objective you are going to achieve. Brainstorm possible solutions ahead of time for any events that may cause you fear.

"Fear is a good thing because it keeps you on your toes and keeps you from being complacent. When fear comes, get out of it quick because if you get stuck in that fear, you get paralyzed."

—Russell Brunson

Chapter 3
FAILURE IS AN OPTION

"We're all going to have setbacks, but you can't let it set you back. What you got to do is decide you're going to go over, under, around or through whatever the obstacle is and get to the other side... Failure's only failure if you let it be. It's always temporary."

—Mark Victor Hansen

ailure is an option! At first glance, this might seem like an unusual comment to make. However, you will discover that millionaires have failed many times but they didn't give up. They were able to perceive their losses as valuable learning experiences which propelled them toward their ultimate success. If you are able to learn from your adversities and keep traveling down the road, you will reach your goals and dreams.

Millionaires view themselves as winners even though they may have failed numerous times. A winner is someone who is persistent in achieving their ambitions despite setbacks. What level of importance are you going to attach to your failure? You have a choice to make. You can either give failure total power over your life or you can take control of your own destiny by interpreting defeat as a lesson to be learned.

It is inevitable that you will face hardships but your ability to maintain a steadfast attitude and continue upward will determine your eventual outcome. In order to increase your chances for victory, throw your ego out the window and realize that it is perfectly acceptable to fail in life. When you achieve your goals, it won't matter how many times you failed. The most important element is that you keep pushing toward your dreams. The only time that a person falls short of becoming a true success is when they give up.

From this point forward, remove all pre-conceived ideas that you have regarding failure. Your past experiences regarding this matter may have shaped your perception up to this point. Negative comments may have been said to you by other people throughout your lifetime in reference to your overall abilities. Perhaps, you may have developed your own misconceptions regarding your past failures. Starting now, give yourself permission to completely erase any negative mindset that you may have when it comes to this entire matter.

Over the years, you may have been brainwashed into thinking that any type of defeat is bad. In reality, it is a good thing because it allows you to learn and grow. It is only harmful if you allow it the chance to prevent you from becoming the incredible person you are meant to be.

To further illustrate this issue, Sean D. Tucker described a life altering event which had a significant impact on his life and career. Several years ago, he was forced to eject from his plane. Sean said, "When I bailed out of my airplane because I couldn't control it, that was a huge failure. I always try to learn from my mistake so I don't repeat it… I try to learn from my failures." Tucker had to confront a major loss but he didn't give up. He was able to acknowledge the setback and learned very quickly how to avoid that problem in the future.

Don't be afraid of failing! Instead, view it as a valuable learning opportunity. When you study highly successful people, you will discover that they were knocked down many times but they continued to persevere. Although failure is one of the greatest challenges we encounter, it is an ordinary part of life. However, if you allow yourself to become consumed with this issue, it will prevent you from moving forward and reaching optimal results. Realize that millionaires encountered failure numerous times but they embraced their hardships with a committed attitude to win. Most importantly, they didn't allow any obstacles to stand in the way of reaching their personal and professional goals.

As a person fails, they are actually becoming more educated and experienced. Understand that every millionaire has dealt with this issue. Some may have filed for bankruptcy or lost their business but they didn't permit this to stop them from being victorious. Instead, these wealthy individuals continued climbing upward due to a firm willpower to succeed.

Remember, when you are confronted by hard times, you have a choice. You can turn and run away or you can push ahead and try again. Continually remind yourself that you need to have the motivation to advance toward your goals. This can be fun, stimulating, and exciting. If you allow yourself to think in those terms, you will joyfully welcome any loss and have fun trying to become victorious. This dedication will bring out your competitive side and then winning will become an exciting goal that you want to achieve.

Simply stated, success becomes a matter of how you are going to interpret your setbacks. If you blow it out of proportion and become very upset over it, then it will stop you in your tracks. However, if you view failure as a challenge to try again, you will move forward. Embrace any hardships with a healthy attitude and realize that these hindrances are only a brief challenge.

The affluent individuals highlighted in this book perceive their failure as being a temporary normal part of life. They embraced their experiences, learned from them, and strived to avoid repeating the same mistakes. The ability to throw doubt out the window and believe in your ability to be triumphant is essential to your victory.

A famous quote by Zig Ziglar stresses the real meaning of failing. Ziglar stated, "Failure is an event, not a person." Failures only represent the results of your actions and don't determine your individual identity or self-worth. This is a critical distinction that needs to be realized in order for you to advance on this life journey both professionally and personally. It doesn't matter what other people may have told you. Disregard any negative statements regarding your past failures. Equally important, don't allow any labels or scripts stored in your subconscious mind to prevent you from taking action and overcoming difficulties. The past is gone forever and today is a brand new start for your positive mindset.

Your inner confidence will soar and a positive self-identity will be established when you know that even though you may have failed, you didn't give up. The decision to keep pushing ahead with a dedicated attitude becomes a vital aspect for your ultimate victory.

Forgiveness for Your Mistakes

When the subject of forgiveness is discussed, the first thought that comes to mind is the idea of forgiving other people for what they have done to you. However, there is another area of forgiveness which is seldom talked about; the ability to forgive yourself for any of your mistakes. As humans, we have a natural tendency to be very hard on ourselves. When people make a mistake, they often put themselves down thereby minimizing their self-esteem. At that moment, it becomes easy to view our abilities in a negative manner. This type of thinking is detrimental and must be changed to a healthier outlook.

Sean D. Tucker stated, "I always try to learn from my mistakes and I always ask forgiveness of myself for my mistakes so I can learn and can forgive myself." If you allow yourself to obsess over a mistake that you made, you will sink into a quicksand of negative emotion. At this point, your subconscious and conscious level will become totally consumed with this issue. When this happens, you will feel defeated and there will be no desire to push ahead.

Sometimes, we criticize ourselves to a point where our self-esteem is totally crushed and becomes non-existent. Regardless of how many times you may have failed, you still need to maintain your dignity, honor, respect, and love for yourself. It is challenging enough to overcome what other people may have said about you. Therefore, you don't need to make it worst by putting yourself down.

The following quick 4-step process will help you move ahead:

1. Acknowledge your mistakes and failures.
2. Forgive yourself.
3. Learn from your failure so that you don't repeat it.
4. Take action and keep accelerating toward your goals.

Learned Helplessness

Psychologists use the term "learned helplessness" to describe a defeatist mentality. In the book, *Learned Optimism: How to Change Your Mind and Your Life*, Martin E. Seligman defines it this way, "Learned helplessness is the giving-up reaction, the quitting response that follows from the belief that whatever you do doesn't matter… Your way of explaining events to yourself determines how helpless you can become, or how energized, when you encounter the everyday setbacks as well as momentous defeats."

Some people just give up when they feel a loss of control. They accept the fact that they are helpless to do anything and their failure becomes a primary focus. On the other hand, if they make a total mind shift and realize that they can seize control over their setback, power returns almost instantaneously and the feeling of helplessness disappears. By continuously reminding yourself that you have power over your life, the eventual outcome will be positive regardless of any hardships.

Release the Negative Script of Failure

Brian Tracy observed, "The fear of failure is a deep subconscious fear that we all develop early in life, usually as the result of destructive criticism." In other words, if you were criticized continually when you were growing up, you will experience fear of failure as an adult until you learn to get rid of it.

During your lifetime, you may have been told that you were a failure. Please stop for a moment! If you were holding onto this negative script throughout your life, it is finally time to release it. Don't allow yourself to be held down by a label that was thrust upon you. As already stated in the Introduction, you need to recognize that the person who sent out this type of energy was an individual who was dealing with their own maladjustment. Some people are miserable and they transmit their own insecurities out to others. In psychology, this is referred to as the concept of transference. The ability to put someone else down gives some people a sense of power and control.

It doesn't matter whether your perception of being a failure comes from a low self-confidence or from other people. You have the authority to release these statements, scripts, and labels out to the universe, up to God, or Jesus.

There may have been a parent, teacher, or another respected person in your life who told you that if you pursued your goals that you would not succeed. They may have crushed your aspirations by strongly encouraging you to pursue another direction. Maybe you took their advice and went down a path you aren't happy with. Realize that you have total power and the time is NOW to change this direction that your life has taken. As long as you hold your dreams within your heart and soul, you will achieve them through dedication, perseverance, and action.

People have been told that they shouldn't try to attain their dreams because of their age, gender, educational level, or background. There are countless individuals, regardless of age, who achieved amazing results. Colonel Sanders, the founder of Kentucky Fried Chicken, and Gene Littlefield, airshow performer, are perfect examples of remarkable individuals who did not allow age to prevent them from achieving their goals. Sanders started to pursue his passion at the age of sixty-five and became very wealthy with his chain of restaurants. At the age of eighty-one, Littlefield graduated from Lewis University in Romeoville, Illinois with a Bachelor of Science Degree in Aviation Maintenance Management. If you consider gender a major barrier for achieving your ambitions, look at Captain Julie Clark. She was one of the very first female commercial airline captains for a major airline. In addition, she became a respected aerobatic pilot in a field that was mostly dominated by men. If you are concerned that your educational background will prevent you from reaching your aspirations, look at Bob Proctor. He was a high school dropout but he didn't allow this to stop him from achieving phenomenal success and becoming a self-made millionaire.

If you want to find excuses for not moving ahead in life; you will. However, if you are willing to embrace your hardships as valuable learning experiences, you will continue onward with a steadfast determination of being triumphant.

You will always find people who will try to discourage you. Don't permit yourself to become consumed with another person's negative outlook. If you really want to pursue your goal, you can find a way. If you allow yourself to find excuses for not pursuing your ambitions, you will remain stuck in life and have remorse in later years. To avoid this, get active and start pushing forward beginning today.

You may not be happy where you are right now in your life but realize that you have the power and capability to achieve any dream or goal that you want. Your past losses don't represent your future success. Instead, learn from your past failures and don't repeat the same mistakes again. If you follow a desire that you hold deep within your heart, you will succeed.

Self-Fulfilling Prophecy

The concept of "self-fulfilling prophecy" was first noted by American sociologist Robert K. Merton. According to Merton, "The self-fulfilling prophecy is, in the beginning, a false definition of the situation evoking a new behavior which makes the originally false conception come true." As described by Merton, a student who feels he is destined to fail a test will spend "more time to worry than to study and then turns in a poor examination." In other words, you will attract into your life whatever you focus on whether it is positive or negative.

Sean D. Tucker discovered that when you are scared, your fearful thoughts will turn into a self-fulfilling prophecy and you will begin to panic. According to Tucker, "If you think negatively; negative stuff is going to happen to you."

This concept also correlates to other areas and it can be a major factor when it comes to your self-image or abilities. If you look at past failures in your life and label yourself as someone who doesn't succeed, you will continue to travel on this life journey with that mentality. On the other hand, if you are willing to make a total mind shift so that you are focused on being prosperous, your future will dramatically change and you will experience amazing results.

When you fail, you are one step closer to achieving whatever you want. In order to overcome setbacks and achieve victory, you simply need to reshape your thinking when you fail at a particular task. Permit yourself to perceive your losses as a valuable learning experience. It will take some time to recondition your thoughts but it can be done and you will be surprised at the results.

Don't get obsessed over a particular loss that you had in the past. Don't be self-critical. At times, you might have the strong inclination to be very hard on yourself. Whenever this happens, challenge yourself and maintain a confident attitude regarding your abilities to achieve whatever you want from life.

The Challenge

"So many people that I know have fear of failure. When I'm going for something, I'm going for something knowing one hundred percent it's going to work. If I do that, I have perfect faith that it's going to work and then I can move mountains to make it happen. The second there is doubt or there is not perfect faith, I get nervous and can't succeed with it. Faith in whatever you're trying to accomplish one hundred percent that you know it's going to work is one of the most important qualities. As soon as doubt creeps in, then everything else slows down and screeches to a halt."

—Russell Brunson

The challenge in life is to continue onward with a persistent attitude even though hardships may be encountered. It is understandable that we may become discouraged when things don't work out but this allows us to rethink the situation and brainstorm possible solutions for becoming triumphant. We don't want to have any regrets because we gave up when things got rough. It is easy to make excuses for not taking action but this will stop us from reaching our dreams and goals in life.

At times, life can be difficult. For some people, it is much easier to give up and live without ambitions. They don't want to face the real world and they allow themselves to become stuck in a protective bubble. As a result, these individuals are living an incomplete life. This life journey is meant to be enjoyed fully and completely. If you want to hide inside your home, you are going to miss the great opportunities that you could truly enjoy. Understand that you have total choice and free will. This means that you can get up right now and start taking action toward your aspirations or you can just sit on the couch watching television and accomplish nothing.

Are you going to fail? Absolutely! But that is ok. You can guarantee your ultimate success by failing. With each loss, you are developing stronger tactics for becoming triumphant. Winners will fail many times but they don't give up. When you study highly admired individuals, you will discover that their losses propelled them to a level that was unbelievable. Allow yourself to take this approach and achieve victory in all areas of your life.

Millionaire System for Overcoming Failure

1. Turn failure into an educational experience.
2. Clear your mind, take a break, and
look again with a refreshed perspective.
3. Create a new solution.

"I think when we can be fully present with the times in which we're failing, and really pull from them lessons of what do and what not to do, how to be, how not to be, how to serve, how not to

*serve; it's in that learning that to me disappointment and failure
is so easily overcome."*

—Brendon Burchard

1. Turn failure into an educational experience

When James Malinchak did a product offering and nobody bought from
him, he turned it into an educational experience from which he was able
to gain a lot of insight. He considered it "one of the greatest things" that
ever happened to him. "I went and learned how to do presentations the
right way that would add value, make a difference, enrich people's lives
but also have them want to continue learning from me," stated James.

Malinchak maintained a positive attitude and reached a healthy
mental state after his initial failure. He didn't take the setback
personally and realized that he could use it as an educational
experience. James evaluated his failure so that he could overcome
the problem that was preventing him from making sales. He took an
objective approach to finding an effective solution. Consequently, his
persistence and willingness to learn from defeat was the catalyst for
skyrocketing his business.

It has been said that if you are not learning in life, then you are not
living or growing. You will find that affluent individuals continue to
develop intellectually. They don't allow themselves to become stagnate
in life and just settle. Instead, they are always pushing toward a goal that
they want to achieve.

When talking to Bob Proctor regarding the issue of dealing with
failure, he stated, "I just get up and keep on going. I've had a lot of
them and I believe they're necessary for you to learn something and
if you're going to keep growing, you're going to keep having failures
because you're not perfect and if you play it safe so that you don't have

failures, then you're stuck. The idea that it's better to be safe than sorry is; it's silly, it's not true at all." Bob went on to say, "I see losing as a part of winning. I see it as a necessary part of winning. You don't necessarily learn from your successes, you learn from the losses. You've got to learn to handle it. You've got to learn to treat it properly. You cannot let it stop you or slow you down."

2. Clear your mind, take a break, and look again with a refreshed perspective

Sometimes, getting away from the office or your home and going for a walk or drive can be very therapeutic and healthy for your mind. If you over analyze any issue, you will not be able to think clearly and find a solution. After this break, you might find that ideas come flowing into your head that you never thought of before.

Taking a break from a particular problem enables you to develop a refreshed perspective and gives the perfect solution a chance to emerge. Some people might want to escape temporarily into their hobby or relieve their stress by spending time in nature. For others, taking a drive can dramatically help to reduce anxiety. If your mind is constantly bombarded with trying to find an answer, you might find that your creative juices stop completely and nothing will be accomplished. For this reason, it is essential to become refreshed and energized with clearly focused thoughts.

After you relax mentally, be open and receptive to the ideas that may flow into your head. You may want to have a pen and paper so that you can write them down. Another great suggestion is to record your thoughts into a digital voice recorder or even your cell phone.

3. Create a new solution

Napolean Hill wrote in *Think and Grow Rich*, "Just keep this fact in mind, and remember when your plans fail, that temporary defeat is not permanent failure. It may only mean that your plans have not been sound. Build other plans."

The importance of being flexible when you are attempting to find the answer to a problem is a critical aspect. Some people are unable to make any type of compromise. The ability to have an open mind and be receptive to all possible solutions is a crucial element for your victory.

According to Mike Filsaime, he did a promotion for a product and it failed. Some people automatically assumed that nobody wanted the product. However, he decided to take another approach by reframing the offer and giving away a free CD. After this, he was able to make the sale by using video. As stated by Mike, "We changed the format, the medium of the marketing message, and repositioned the message." Surprisingly, the product never changed and it went on to do over a million dollars in sales. Over two years, it did two million dollars. As a result, Filsaime stated that "failure is a good thing."

After you have removed yourself mentally from the issue, return at a later point and look at the situation from a completely refreshed perspective. At this point, bring your team members together and concentrate on how you can solve the problem. Brainstorm with them and discover alternatives that you may never have imagined. By opening yourself up to help from your employees, you can get everyone's feedback and opinions.

Lessons Learned

"In everything we do, there's going to be a rhythm; there's going to be an up and down. In order for it to go up a little bit, it's going to have to go down at some time because it is the laws of nature… In order for me to have a success, I'm going to need some failures. I cannot be successful with every single thing… With failure, there's knowledge gained from the experience… You have to be able to

go back and say: 1. Here's what I learned. 2. What can I apply
for success?"

—Mike Filsaime

According to James Malinchak, "How do you deal with failure? It's a very simple line: you've got to get up when life knocks you down; the only way that you fail in this world is if you decide to quit and give up. Understand that failure, roadblocks, and obstacles are just part of the process; it's what you choose to do... You just got to think that failures aren't the end of all; it's just a learning process."

Understand that failure does not represent your ability to achieve success; it does not determine your self-worth as an individual. If you allow failure to stop you from taking further action, then you will not proceed or move forward in life. At that point, you will become stagnate and will never accomplish your dreams. But if you choose to move ahead, the difficulties you experience can become your chance to learn and grow.

By closely examining effective strategies from highly respected millionaires, you will find that they use failure to devise effective solutions to their problem. In talking with Russell Brunson, he sums up the entire issue very precisely by stating, "Usually failures are like ninety-nine percent there, there's just a tweak or a change or something you do a little differently. As soon as you see that angle and figure it out, you can change a failure to success very, very quickly."

You may not succeed with a given task but this does not represent your self-worth as a unique individual. By acquiring knowledge from your losses and using them as a learning experience, you are opening yourself up to becoming a true winner in life. All of those failures just mean you are that much closer to winning.

Failure is an ordinary part of life and you shouldn't be self-critical regarding your abilities when you fail. Through the hardships, you are actually becoming much stronger and learning effective strategies that will help you. Highly respected leaders and entrepreneurs have failed many times but they didn't give up and walk away.

You may fail over and over again but as long as you keep pushing forward and don't give up, your inner confidence will strengthen. If you make the decision now, you can pursue your goals even if you gave up on them because of a past loss. Maybe your emotional growth was stunted and you became frozen at a particular stage along your path. Now is the time to make a total mind shift and allow yourself to be inspired by the millionaires in this book. As long as you still have your dream deep within your heart and soul, get active and start moving in a direction that will get you to your ultimate goal.

Life is going to pass by and you should live it fully. Realize that you will fail and that is ok. We all make mistakes but that is how we learn better tactics for being successful. So, failure is an option that should be embraced openly. You don't want to have any regrets because you gave up when life became difficult. Keep a committed attitude to succeed and learn from your mistakes. With this positive outlook, you are helping to ensure your victory.

On this life journey, you should always be advancing forward with your emotional development; you are the only person who has the power to stop your growth! Don't let failure hold you back! Other people might discourage you but ultimately, you make the decision to move ahead or become stuck.

Master Mind Action Steps

Action Step #1: Take out a piece of paper and draw a line down the middle. On one side of the column, write down where your plan failed. In the other column, write down what you are going to do in order to avoid that failure in the future.

Action Step #2: For this action step, do the following:

1. Get involved with your hobby.
2. Spend time with your children, family, and friends.
3. Go for a walk or drive.
4. Completely clear your mind.
5. Give your mind a break and a chance to get refreshed.

Action Step #3: Take another sheet of paper and get creative. Write down all possible solutions for the failure that you experienced. If you have team members, encourage their active participation during this brainstorming activity. Allow all ideas to flow openly.

"Is cheating somebody out of something a failure? Is humiliating somebody because it feels good a failure? Is demeaning or maligning somebody's character a failure? If you fail as a human being, that's truly a failure. If you fail financially, so what? You didn't cheat anybody."

—**Sean D. Tucker**

Chapter 4

IMPORTANCE OF HAVING A MENTOR OR COACH

"I may not even be alive today if it wasn't for mentors or coaches. I think they're absolutely essential. They're a prerequisite in any kind of success. You can't do it on your own. Nobody's ever done anything of any consequence on their own."

—Bob Proctor

I n this chapter, you are going to learn an inside secret that has been well-guarded for many years. Generally, this golden nugget is not released to the public but the millionaires spotlighted within the pages of this book were completely honest and shared this information to help you. Revealed within this chapter is a major factor of their blueprint for success. This critical element involves the importance of having a mentor or coach who can guide you so that your path to success is significantly shortened.

Throughout this book, you are being given direct access to eight millionaires who are providing their own form of coaching with you one-on-one.

Here is a breakdown of the different models of the mentoring process:

1. Find a mentor or coach who can guide and inspire you.
2. Become involved in a master mind group with like-minded people.
3. Invest in a home study course.
4. Attend seminars.
5. Read books.

Having direct interaction with an adviser and master mind group is at the top of the list.

You might be wondering what a master mind group involves. Generally, it is a group of individuals with similar goals who come together to help each other with their business and personal objectives. If the members are active, they can help you brainstorm solutions, give you encouragement, and hold you accountable for taking action. Even though a master mind might be focused on business or financial aspects, people can gain emotional support from each other. When you have encouragement and guidance from other members, your desire to achieve your objectives will be greatly enhanced.

In order to ensure your ultimate victory, you need to seek out experts within your given industry. This is one of the most effective strategies utilized by the inner circle of millionaires. They don't allow their pride to prevent them from reaching out to others for help and guidance. Yet, there are some people who refuse to get any assistance from coaches who are more experienced. As a result, they struggle every week to survive and some of them will face bankruptcy. Appreciate the fact that a trusted adviser can dramatically influence your business and personal life in tremendous ways. In some cases, a deep friendship or business partnership may develop.

Realize that you don't have to do everything on your own. In fact, the most successful people in the world have consultants to guide them along the way but they usually don't advertise this information to the general public.

Are you willing to get help in achieving your personal and business goals? Be receptive to the lessons that you can learn from others who have more knowledge. They can provide you with a step-by-step plan for victory and you can save a lot of time with their assistance. If you allow your pride to prevent you from using the guidance of a mentor or coach, you are not acting in your best interest.

Recognize that prosperous individuals build off the expertise from others. Are you familiar with Orville and Wilbur Wright? They were two brothers and inventors who built the very first airplane that was able to fly. All of the aviators and aeronautical engineers who came after the Wright Brothers continued to advance the initial design from the first airplane. They didn't go back and try to rediscover the entire concept of flight. Instead, they continued to build from an original concept and proven formula.

All of the millionaires who were interviewed for this book welcomed the support from trusted advisers. This is one success strategy that needs to be incorporated into your life. Why go through the hardship of attempting to do everything by yourself when you can get assistance from others who are more experienced? The amount of time and energy that you can save through the implementation of this highly effective strategy can skyrocket your life. If you examine top performing athletes, actors, musical artists, or business executives, you will find that they openly receive coaching in order to help them excel within their profession.

Reach out to people who are knowledgeable and can help you within your business and personal life. Learn from their experiences and make your own path a little bit easier. They can give you shortcuts and secrets that could increase your finances in ways you never thought possible. It is truly amazing what a trusted consultant can help you with if you allow them that opportunity.

The Challenge

"I surround myself with experts in areas of domain in which I want to master and I surround myself with a group of guys and gals who, in a mastermind, we share our ideas with. We learn from each other. We extend and challenge each other, and so I'm constantly surrounded by other people who are giving me feedback, who are telling me what I can try, where I can go, and who are checking me if they ever see something they don't like."

—Brendon Burchard

The willingness to obtain help from a trusted coach is the utmost importance in accelerating your movement forward on the road to being triumphant. Equally important, the ability to gain additional guidance from master mind groups, home study courses, seminars, and books should be fully embraced with an open attitude. Using a combination of these methods will lead to substantial results.

A valuable mentor is someone who can share their knowledge and insight with you. This should be someone who is willing to challenge you and be firm with you so that you can start moving forward. You don't want someone who is going to agree with everything you say just because you are paying them for their advice.

Millionaire System for Having a Mentor or Coach

1. Find a mentor or coach.
2. Become a member of a master mind group.
3. Invest in continuing education with
home study courses, seminars, and books.

"Really appreciate having that mentorship... It short cuts so much time when you have someone there that can steer you in the right direction."

—Russell Brunson

1. Find a mentor or coach

When you are attempting to locate a mentor or coach, you will have to do your homework and research. This is a very serious issue and should not be taken lightly. Seek out people who are experienced within the given area that you want to master. You may not be able to get direct access to the top experts within your industry. But, you can still invest in their books, home study courses, or attend their seminars. This provides another great way to learn from them. Realize that a consultant can be your key to amazing success.

If you want direct coaching from a highly respected and well-known expert, be willing to make a financial investment. If a highly regarded individual can propel you to six or seven figures a year in salary by using their techniques, what is that worth? Naturally, they can't guarantee your results but they can significantly increase your probability of being successful. It is not being suggested that you go into extreme debt in order to get a valuable consultant. However, realize that investing in your future is worthwhile. For this reason, pick your adviser very carefully. It is important to select someone who has a proven track record of generating substantial and tangible results. Ultimately, your outcome, either positive or negative, is based upon the decisions that you make and your willingness to take action.

2. Become a member of a master mind group

The amount of guidance, support, and information that you can gain from a master mind group is amazing. Under this model, a group of people will share ideas with other members. This can be accomplished through conference calls, forums, emails, and meeting in person. The ability to brainstorm with other members can accelerate your progress forward. As a result, you will discover effective strategies for reaching your business and personal goals.

There may be people in your life who don't understand your dreams. For this reason, a master mind group can be a great asset especially when you realize that other individuals have overcome the same obstacles that you are trying to push through.

Receiving encouragement from other people who have similar ambitions can be a major help in giving you that extra push forward. Sometimes, family members, friends, and co-workers are unable to comprehend what you are attempting to accomplish because of their own limited perspective. They may not believe it is possible for you to reach your aspirations so they may project that negative view onto you. But when you are able to share ideas with people who have the same mindset, this source of positive energy can greatly benefit you.

Master mind group members openly share their tips, strategies, and techniques with each other. Sometimes, the support from other members can help to motivate and inspire you to your highest level of excellence.

3. Invest in continuing education with home study courses, seminars, and books

We are going to examine three areas of continuing education:

1. Home Study Courses
2. Seminars
3. Books

Home Study Courses

Home study courses can provide access to top experts within a given industry and they can give you a competitive advantage in gaining valuable information. They are a great resource because you can advance through them at your own pace and convenience. Also, you can easily go back and review the material.

Seminars

Seminars represent an engaging and stimulating opportunity to gain more knowledge within a certain field. You are able to meet with respected experts and learn their secrets. Also, seminars give you the chance to socialize and network with other people.

Let's take a look at some of the seminars offered by the millionaires featured in this book:

- Brendon Burchard hosts the "Experts Academy" and "High Performance Academy" seminars. Experts Academy is considered to be the most comprehensive marketing training for authors, speakers, coaches, and online thought leaders. Burchard teaches people how to position themselves as a highly paid expert in any topic area. With the High Performance Academy, Brendon provides the world's most comprehensive motivation and high performance training for achievers.

- James Malinchak hosts the "Big Money Speaker Boot Camp" where he provides speaker training to anyone interested in living their mission, making a positive difference, and changing the world while making a great living. Also, he hosts the "College Speaking Success Boot Camp" where he teaches people how they can have a lucrative career speaking on college and university campuses.
- Steve Harrison hosts the "National Publicity Summit" where he invites over 100 producers and journalists from America's top media outlets to meet with attendees one-on-one.

At times, the other highlighted millionaires featured in this book may host a seminar, workshop or be an invited speaker at another event.

Do your research and find a seminar that is closely related to what you want to master. When you attend a seminar in person, the level of excitement is phenomenal. People have a tendency to become very passionate and energetic. Often, they are ready to take immediate action.

However, when the attendees leave the seminar and go back home, the enthusiasm seems to disappear. They sometimes feel alone in the pursuit of their goals especially if they don't have much support within their immediate circle of family and friends. The motivation to push for their dreams is now gone. As a result, when you are at the seminar, network with the other attendees and develop your own master mind group to help each other after the event is over. This will help to ensure that you keep your goals paramount and the other members can challenge you to take action. If you go home and feel discouraged, you will have a support system that you can reach out to. As a result, you won't feel alone and you'll realize that you can achieve your dreams.

Books

Books can also play an important role in the mentoring process. James Malinchak has become a respected millionaire and appeared on ABC's television show, *"Secret Millionaire."* However, years ago, he was a sales representative who was trying to become a financial consultant. James recalled, "I didn't have any money; I was broke. I couldn't afford anything." He would sit in the Barnes and Noble bookstore in Pasadena, California every Friday, Saturday, and most of Sunday. Malinchak said, "I would sit there and read and devour every sales book that I could because I couldn't afford to buy them."

When you study highly successful people, you will find that they are able to get creative and always seek alternatives for achieving their ambitions. The dedication and commitment shown by Malinchak was a critical aspect for his success. James didn't have any money to purchase a book but he didn't let this issue stop him. Instead, he went to the bookstore and started reading books so that he could learn and grow.

If you are limited on financial resources, don't let this delay your training. Permit yourself to use the same technique that James used and go to the book store. Also, you can go to your local library and do research on the internet. However, a word of caution about using the internet. There is a lot of false and misleading information that can send you in the wrong direction; be sure that you seek out reliable sources.

When Malinchak began his journey, he wasn't coached directly by a mentor but still gained valuable information from all the books that he read. They provided him the opportunity to learn from experts. As a result, he views books and CDs as important mentoring tools. "Mentoring can be through books, through CDs; to be masterminding in a group with other like-minded people," said James.

Allow yourself to be inspired by James Malinchak and don't make excuses for not taking action. Challenge yourself to find innovative ways to make your plan work. When you start taking action, you will find amazing opportunities.

Similarly, Bob Proctor also recognizes the importance that books can play on the educational journey. For instance, he has read *Think and Grow Rich* by Napolean Hill countless times. According to Proctor, "I want to grow. I want to do bigger things and do better things... We keep studying, we keep growing and as we grow, we develop a greater awareness. So we see more and we're aware of more than we were before. And we find bigger and better ways to do things, to make things happen. I'll study forever."

If you are actively involved in learning on a consistent basis, your mind will be stimulated allowing you to achieve astonishing results. Continuing education is a critical element for your eventual victory. By seeking out guidance from mentors, coaches, master mind groups, and books, you are continuing forward with a non-stoppable momentum.

Lessons Learned

> *"A mentor is going to help you, assist you, and guide you. They're going to help you along the way to avoid mistakes... There are people to mentor or help you to: 1. Increase your chances of success. 2. Give you a shortened learning curve. 3. Give you an accelerated learning program... It is important to have a mentor and look to somebody who has walked in the footsteps already. I've had many mentors and coaches and will continue to have them."*
>
> **—Mike Filsaime**

Do you want to shorten your learning curve and accelerate your progress? In order to accomplish this goal, it is important to get guidance from a trusted source that can help you avoid mistakes and achieve success. There is no reason for you to start from the very beginning when there are highly qualified individuals who can greatly assist you.

All of the millionaires in this book respect the importance of having a mentor or coach to guide them. They don't allow their pride to prevent them from getting help and reaching out to advisers. Admit that you don't know everything and welcome assistance from other people who are more experienced.

You have a choice to make. If you decide to be stubborn and refuse help, your chances of victory will be reduced. However, if you are open to getting a consultant, you will greatly increase your probability of being victorious. Your search for an adviser should be done with careful research and study. You should look for someone who can inspire and challenge you. Ongoing support from an expert within your field and master mind groups will give you a great advantage in being successful.

Mastermind Action Steps

Action Step #1: Start researching experts, mentors, and coaches within your given industry. Make a list of the people you would like to work with and reach out to them. Before you contact them, have a list of questions written out that you can ask them. You are going to be interviewing the mentors to see if you want to have them for your coach.

Trust your intuition and choose the best consultant that you feel is going to help you reach optimal results.

Action Step #2: Look into master mind groups that can help you. Write out a list of groups that you would like to join as a member. Contact them and ask the following questions:

- How many members do you currently have?
- How active are your members?
- Do I have email and phone access to everyone?

- Is there a forum where I can post questions?
- Do you have conference calls with the members?
- Is there an opportunity to meet with other members in person?

Action Step #3: Find home study courses, seminars, and books that can assist you in achieving your business and personal goals. This is a great action step if you want to learn more from a highly respected expert or guru within your industry.

"I believe anything you want to do; you must go and invest with somebody who's already figured it out. Mentor with them, let them mentor you and coach you, and know they will save ninety percent off your learning curve."

—**James Malinchak**

Chapter 5
HAVING PERSISTENCE AND PUSHING FORWARD

"I think what people must do is clarify: What is their highest ambition of who they want to be? What they want to achieve? What they want to give... What makes life meaningful and fulfilling is that sense that we are progressing towards something that's important to us. Without persistence, without dedication, without constancy, then what do we have? We have meandering, we have delay, we have boredom... A life of action, a life of dedication, a life of constancy towards something that we believe to be meaningful... We're dedicated to it, then life opens."

—Brendon Burchard

Reaching your dreams isn't going to be easy. You are going to encounter setbacks and get knocked down several times. However, as long as you keep getting up and moving ahead, nothing will prevent you from ultimate victory. If you maintain persistence and push forward with a steadfast attitude, you will succeed.

If you want anything worthwhile in life, you are going to have to work for it. Even though it may not be what people like to hear, you have to get active in order to reach the goals that you want to achieve. In time, you will discover that the obstacles and hardships you encounter are easier to overcome. Through this process, you will develop a tremendous amount of self-esteem and improved self-worth when you are actively working on achieving your goals.

Understand that millionaires maintain dedication and the willingness to work for their emotional and financial success. Prosperity and happiness didn't magically appear just because they wanted it. They developed a strategic plan and took action in order to become successful. For them, watching television, surfing the internet for countless hours, and concentrating on nonproductive activities was not an option. To the contrary, their attention was focused on high-priority tasks that propelled them toward their aspirations.

There is no magic button that can be pushed to get a dream house, dream car, a perfect relationship, or all of the money that you want. Anyone who tells you this is lying to you. Throughout this book, you are being provided with proven strategies that, if implemented and utilized on a regular basis, will produce substantial results in all areas of your life. These tactics are a well-organized and systematic process that can bring wealth and contentment if you follow them. When you have a willingness and dedication to work toward your ambitions, you will attain them.

With the "law of attraction" principle, you will attract into your life whatever your attention is focused on. Simply put, if you send out positive energy and thoughts to the universe, you will get back the same. However, this does not mean that you can lie in bed all day and expect money to drop into your lap. You have to get up and take action while you are simultaneously sending out the positive energy to the universe. You are rewarded in life for taking action and not giving up. You are going to be thrown challenges but this is when you must maintain a strong willpower to persist and push ahead.

Self-esteem and self-worth are necessary elements for a healthy mind. Well, how can you feel self-confident if you give up when presented with a setback? The ability to keep pushing onward with persistence when faced with failure and fear is critical to reaching success.

Indecisiveness, hesitation, and the decision to do nothing will completely stop you from advancing forward. As a result, you will stop growing emotionally, intellectually, and financially. Do you really want that for your life? You have been given a great gift; the power of having free will and the ability to make choices. By sitting back and letting life pass you by, you are making a decision. In order to feel fulfilled, you need to go after your dreams and goals. If you are willing to work for your objectives, you will reach them and achieve inner satisfaction and happiness.

Up to this point, you may have encountered hardships. Recognize that your past is gone forever. However, you have the ability to change your future beginning from this moment forward. Living in the past is a total waste of time. Your focus should be on the present and future. The past can't be changed but your future can be shaped in the direction that you want. Believe it or not, you can change your life beginning today in a totally new direction. You might be unsure how to accomplish this new way of thinking. Allow the information in this book to be the catalyst that will propel you to the highest possible level that you can reach. You have free will, total choice over your life, and the power inside your heart and soul to reach all of your aspirations.

At times, it is possible to become locked into a negative event that happened in our past. When this happens, it is the equivalent to being in quicksand and you will sink deeper into a negative state of mind. To avoid this, release the past and center your attention on the present and the future.

How important is it for you to reach your dreams? Let's take a look at Mark Victor Hansen and Jack Canfield. They had a strong desire to get their book published but they had a major challenge. They contacted over a 140 publishers before a small publishing company agreed to publish *Chicken Soup for the Soul.* Subsequently, the book was published, turned into a series, and sold millions of copies. What was the key element to their success? Hansen and Canfield kept persisting until they found a publishing company that would publish *Chicken Soup for the Soul.* Within their framework, giving up was never an option. Their dream of getting the book published was the motivation that allowed them to persevere even though they received rejection after rejection. Their only option was success and they transmitted this message and energy out to the universe. They kept taking action until they found a publishing company that would work with them.

How many people would have the same level of persistence as Hansen and Canfield? It was extremely challenging to keep persisting but they never gave up. Their goal of getting published was so strong that nothing could stop them. You will discover that people who become prosperous all have this same type of mindset. They don't permit hardships to stop them from achieving their ambitions. If you are receptive, you can incorporate this same attitude into your life. It may take some practice but it can be accomplished.

Think about this. If you sit back and let life pass you by, you will never accomplish anything of significance. You have a purpose, dreams, and goals. You have a gift or message to share with the world and other people. You are meant to be happy and reach all of your wishes. Get clearly focused on what you really want to achieve, get dedicated, have perseverance, and start taking action today.

Recognize that you are going to hit roadblocks along your path but if you keep accelerating onward with a determined attitude, nothing will stop you and success will be attained. The ability to have dedication and persistence will be a golden key that will unlock tremendous rewards for you.

The Challenge

"I am very persistent. I'm not persistent by accident. I'm persistent by design. If you're not persistent, you're not going to win because no one's smart enough to do it right the first time, and you've got to keep doing it until you get it right. If you can see something in your mind, if you can see it finished, then there is a way to do it, and so you've got to persist. Persistence! It's absolutely essential and you can develop it!"

—Bob Proctor

Time continues to pass by on a daily basis. You can just settle for what you currently have or you can start moving forward. The choice is totally up to you. You can live a life of mediocrity and complacency or one of vibrancy and energy through action. Once you start your momentum onward, it will become accelerated over time and generate substantial results.

Millionaires have faced obstacles countless times. However, their perception regarding these challenges has allowed them to overcome barriers with a healthy mental attitude. They don't obsess over the failures that they encounter. To the contrary, they view them as being an ordinary part of life that can be used as a valuable training lesson.

At times, when faced with fear and failure, it might appear easier to give up and walk away. But, this will create an emotional defeat and self-confidence will be diminished. The true test of winning is the ability to persevere and have a strong dedication to reach your objectives even though you endure hardships.

A large number of people focus on a loss as being bad and they might start to blame themselves for what happened. However, millionaires have a different mental attitude regarding this issue. They don't interpret failure as a negative aspect. They view it as an educational experience in which they can grow. There is no time for them to obsess over the hardships that they encounter. To the contrary, they view them as a normal part of life and they continue to push forward because they are focused on their final objective.

Russell Brunson observed, "The majority of my peers are gone, they've disappeared because they didn't have that perseverance... when the fight came, they just walked away." Russell took a different approach than his colleagues. He was willing push through rough times in order to reach his ultimate goal. Understand that a person gains true respect, honor, and dignity when they are able to accept any type of defeat and keep pushing onward with a firm commitment to succeed.

If you allow yourself to surrender to any type of loss, you will not achieve your ambitions in life. As a result, you will not feel a sense of accomplishment.

You don't want to look back on your life and feel any regrets for not attempting to reach your aspirations. If you tried many times and failed over and over, you can still feel fulfilled. If you encountered defeat and gave up, you will feel like a failure. In reality, what have you got to lose? Go after your dreams and goals with a strong willpower. If you get knocked down along the way, get up and keep going. At least you will have inner peace and satisfaction knowing that you kept pushing ahead.

The adversities that you encounter in life will make you stronger and can add to your success in the future. If you are willing to take action and persevere through the challenging times, you will be rewarded in the long run.

Millionaire System for Having Persistence and Pushing Forward

1. Pursue your highest ambition;
clarify what you want to achieve.
2. Don't give up; don't walk away.
3. Schedule your projects on a calendar;
promise a completion date.

"Every single day I have the persistence to commit myself to excellence. I understand life is precious. I'm not guaranteed tomorrow. I'm guaranteed this moment. If you live it joyfully, you live it with reverence and passion. When I wake up, my persistence is what I think is the key to my success. When you live life joyfully, it's contagious and other people are attracted to that, and they want to be around you because you're joyful. Everybody is searching for joy in life, not pleasure. True happiness is a joyful existence and experience."

—Sean D. Tucker

1. Pursue your highest ambition; clarify what you want to achieve

When you are deciding what you should do, center your attention on pursuing your highest ambition. What do you really want to accomplish? Spend serious consideration on this matter and clearly define what you want to achieve.

We all have aspirations. However, for some people, these dreams and goals have been pushed to the side and are not foremost within their conscious mind. This is the time to get refocused on what you really want to have in your life both professionally and personally. What are your goals that you always wanted to achieve? Maybe roadblocks were thrown into your path and you didn't know how to navigate around them. Throughout the pages of this book, you have a detailed plan for overcoming any challenges which may arise on your life journey.

If you have given up on your ambitions, there is a part of you that is not thriving. You may find yourself going day-to-day just doing the same old things out of habit. At times, life can become very routine, boring, and dull when you aren't pursuing your dreams. People sometimes allow themselves to fall into this trap and become very complacent. However, this is not truly living. Life should be lived vibrantly and energetically with a strong enthusiasm and passion for reaching your aspirations. This passion for living enthusiastically and achieving your objectives may be buried deep within your soul but it is time to bring it up to the surface on a conscious level. This life journey can be fun and exciting if you are willing to take action. Setbacks and failures will come as a part of the process but you can use them as a learning experience which will make you stronger and get you to your ultimate dreams.

The key element to reaching a high level of success is to keep growing and expanding. Don't let life pass you by. Your persistence will be much stronger if you are working toward your ultimate goals.

2. Don't give up; don't walk away

Make a promise to yourself that you will stay committed to reaching whatever you want from life. If you abandon your goals, you will never know if you could have achieved them. If you keep trying, the potential for victory remains open. In time, you might be very surprised at what happens. The creative side of your brain will become engaged and you will find innovative ways to reach your dreams despite setbacks. For this reason, perseverance is critical for your eventual success.

Realize that people who give up and walk away from their ambitions never reach them. This might seem like an obvious statement to make but it is important to recognize this point on a conscious level. We all have human emotions and when it gets rough in life, we might want to run away. However, these are the times that you have to get even more committed to reaching your aspirations. They are within your heart and soul. If you take action, you will reach your objectives. If you don't do anything, then you will not receive anything back. From this moment forward, keep pushing ahead with a determined and committed attitude of being successful.

Imagine this. If you have an employee who is highly dedicated and always working diligently to ensure that they go above and beyond their job description, they will be a great asset for your company. On the other hand, if you have another employee who does the bare minimum to get by, this person will not receive much respect. When an opportunity arises for a promotion within your company, who are you going to promote and reward? Of course, you will reward the employee who went that extra mile for you. Likewise, you are also rewarded in life for becoming actively engaged.

Visualizing your dreams as if you are living them now and posting images of your goals on a dream board can be that extra motivation to help you overcome any challenging times.

3. Schedule your projects on a calendar; promise a completion date

By scheduling your projects on a calendar, you are holding yourself accountable for getting things done. When you assign a completion date to your projects, there is a psychological element that will become activated and you know that it must be finished. As a result, you will do what it takes to accomplish the task by that date. Even though you may encounter challenges and setbacks, you brush them off and keep moving forward with a determined attitude. Simply put, the date on the calendar is your motivating force for finishing the assignment. This can be the catalyst that will launch you toward reaching any goal or dream that you may have.

Think back to when you were in school or when a supervisor gave you an assignment to complete. When you had a deadline and a predetermined date of completion, you became activated and got it done. You didn't make any excuses. You were totally focused on completing the project.

Lessons Learned

"Persistence is going to be based on both successes and failures. The more success you have, the easier it is to continue and you'll persist because of the fruits of the labor. If you're persisting and you continue to fail, that's when you have to be willing to adapt. As long as you know you are making progress every day, going in the right direction, and looking at everything objectively; persistence is key... Make sure that you get the rewards of all your hard work by enjoying life with your family, significant other, the kids, and certainly your friends."

—Mike Filsaime

Your will! Your desire to succeed! Your willingness to take action! These are essential qualities that you must maintain in order to be triumphant.

It is very important to have persistence and be willing to push forward without allowing a negative view from someone else or a particular event to stop you. This sense of perseverance will uniquely establish you as a person who will be very successful both professionally and personally.

Writing down your goals and having a completion date will give you that extra motivation to keep moving ahead. When you do this, there is no choice of giving up. Your only option will be to complete your task.

Master Mind Action Steps

Action Step #1: Write down your goals and dreams. Let your creative juices and energy flow. Put in writing whatever comes into your mind first and get all of your ideas down on paper. You might want to take your time so that you don't overwhelm yourself when you look at your final list. When you are done, you can go back and prioritize them. Number your goals by importance.

Action Step #2: Don't walk away from the pursuit of your goals. Even though there are challenges, stay in the game. Take a list of your written dreams and tape them in a location where you will see them on a daily basis. You want to be reminded every day of what you are going to accomplish in life. Also, post them on a dream board. This will be a constant reminder of what you are pushing for.

Action Step #3: Get a calendar and post it on your wall or door. For each of your objectives, write them on a given date that you want to have them finished. As you complete each task on your calendar, put a check mark next to them.

"Persistence is critically important. If projects don't get scheduled and put on a calendar, they'll tend not to get done. Another way to be persistent is to have a grid of the people that you want to follow up with and you put their name on the grid. You just simply mark: Did you get a yes or no decision? I call this a relationship grid. These are the people that you want to connect with and keep persisting until you get a yes or a no. Your job is to persist until you get a decision."

—Steve Harrison

Chapter 6
MINDSET FOR SUCCESS

"I think it's celebrating the magnificence of life through your work, through your love, through your relationships, and celebrating the magnificence of the joyfulness of life... I'm going to do the best of my abilities to have an empowering day today. I am going to make this work. I'm going to be good for this world. I'm going to make it a better place, and I'm going to be as positive as I can, instead of dwelling on the negatives. If you're joyful and happy in your life, you're empowered because the essence of life is so important."

—Sean D. Tucker

When you begin to analyze all of the success tactics outlined in this book, the mindset strategy is, by far, the most important. How can millionaires consistently achieve success over and over again? They are able to maintain a firm belief that nothing will stop them from reaching their eventual goals and dreams.

They don't allow failures or setbacks to shape their individual identity. At the same time, they view adversities as both a normal part of life and the opportunity to attain intellectual growth and development. When faced with any challenge, there is only one option for these millionaires; the ability to maintain a positive attitude regardless of what obstacles are thrown into their path.

Your mental perception of what you can accomplish is very powerful. Your mindset can shape your entire life. By integrating a winning mentality into your daily routine, you can excel in all areas. Above all, you must develop and maintain a firm belief in yourself. Yes, you have to believe in yourself and realize that you can achieve victory.

All of the highly respected individuals who attained the status of becoming prosperous maintained a confident attitude on a daily basis. In a manner of speaking, it is a positive vibrational energetic level that continues to expand and grow continuously which allows them to reach a higher level of emotional and intellectual development. Even though these affluent individuals may encounter some turbulence on their daily flight through life, they endure it knowing that their eventual goal will be the pot of gold at the end of the rainbow.

How does a millionaire differ from someone who hasn't made that leap? They incorporate a step-by-step plan into their daily routine. This plan includes the following eight steps:

1. Be firmly committed to reach all your dreams and goals.
2. Maintain the driving force to push through challenges, obstacles, and failures.
3. Keep a positive attitude with the realization that success will be achieved.
4. Be thankful for what you currently have in your life and have gratitude for what you will receive.
5. Develop affirmations that are focused on your aspirations.

6. Have a dream board and visualize your goals as if you have them now.
7. Implement the eight success strategies into your life.
8. Be willing to take decisive action every day.

Your thoughts will determine your eventual victory. After you are able to elevate yourself to a higher intellectual level, no challenge or setback can stop you from reaching your ambitions. It is simply a matter of prioritizing your objectives. When you are open and receptive to this concept, a new level of consciousness will be triggered that will allow you to attain whatever you want.

It is inevitable that everyone will experience obstacles and failures. However, how is a prosperous individual able to handle these experiences? They are able to embrace these challenges and realize that they are only temporary and will eventually disappear. They understand that hardships are just an educational experience. When you are able to incorporate this same level of awareness into your daily routine, advancement toward your aspirations will become accelerated and the energy level that you feel throughout your body will be transmitted out to the world. This feeling at the conscious level will permeate into your subconscious level and there will be an eventual merging of each one. When this happens, the commitment that you have for reaching your objectives will be rock solid.

Even though you might not feel it totally right now, the time has come for you to change your past thinking. Deep down, you have a desire to change your life in a positive direction. We are all meant to be happy and live life with passion. Understand that there are going to be momentary hardships but that does not determine your identity or destiny.

Some people become so consumed with failure that it becomes the only issue they can focus on. On the other hand, when successful individuals experience difficulties, they don't view them as a problem. They openly embrace them as an ordinary part of living and comprehend that adversities will fade away. With a committed attitude, perseverance, and dedication, anyone can proceed forward through any obstacle. Most importantly, you can model the exact same steps that have been used by millionaires in order to accomplish your greatest ambitions.

If you choose to do nothing, there will be no opportunity for growth or emotional development. It is part of our human condition to learn, to advance, and to become involved with continuing education. When you stop growing intellectually, there is no movement, no joy, no passion, and no excitement. You will wither away emotionally. Don't allow yourself to fall into this negative trap.

Millionaires have a passion, excitement, and joy for life. They understand that there will be good and bad times but that's ok. Likewise, when you are able to comprehend this concept, you realize that the good times far outweigh any bad times. You don't want to have any remorse for not taking action and trying to reach all of your dreams and goals. We all need to go out and try to attain our aspirations. You may fall down along the way but that's ok. When you look back on your life, you don't want to say that "I should have" or "what if." Instead, you want to say, "I did it. I never gave up. I had the firm willpower to achieve my dreams."

To illustrate the power of having the right mindset, Bob Proctor went to Prudential Insurance in downtown Chicago and he met with the Vice President of Sales. Proctor asked to work with a hundred of his best sales people and he told him that he would help them improve their sales. Well, he helped them to improve their sales by "hundreds of millions of dollars" which was truly astonishing.

How in the world was Bob able to make such a dramatic difference to their sales revenue? "I showed them how to change their paradigms; showed them how to change their conditioning. I said your programs sell what you're selling. If you don't change the program, you're never going to change. I got them focused. What are they doing at nine o'clock in the morning? They were going to their office. What for? You're not selling to anybody there. You're not selling insurance to insurance people. Get up! Get in front of somebody that needs insurance. Ask them to buy. So, I got them convinced to get in front of somebody before nine am," said Proctor. As the result of Bob's innovative approach, they were selling more hundred thousand dollar policies in a week than they previously sold in a year in every office.

Millionaire ABC Mindset

Here are the three essential qualities of the millionaire mindset:

ACTION – Take consistent and decisive action on a continuous basis.

BELIEF – Believe in yourself. You can accomplish any goal or dream that you desire.

COMMITMENT – Be firmly committed on a daily basis to reaching your aspirations.

The Challenge

"The millionaire mindset realizes you don't have to get it perfect; you just have to get it out there. Have it good enough to get started. Test things knowing that you can adjust them and improve them as you go."

—Steve Harrison

Sometimes, our limited thinking and the advice from other people prevents us from progressing forward. Remember, your mental perception of what you want to achieve will determine your eventual outcome. If you truly hold a dream deep within your heart and soul, you will accomplish it with a dedicated attitude of being successful and taking action. Don't allow a limited mindset to prevent you from reaching any goal or dream that you may have.

When you were a child, you most likely believed that you could have anything in the world. However, at some point in your life, you established a blocking mechanism which completely crushed your unlimited earning potential and the ability to reach a total abundance of emotional peace, harmony, and happiness. Why did you put up this blocker? Maybe you felt that your original goals and dreams weren't possible and were unrealistic.

Realize that other people had similar dreams and they didn't give up. You can attain whatever you want if you are able to release that blocking mechanism which is stopping you. Release your limiting beliefs and understand that you can reach anything that you want.

One way you can take charge of your own subconscious beliefs is through affirmations. To do this, get out a piece of paper and write down a complimentary statement about yourself or something you want to achieve. For example, here is an affirmation from Bob Proctor for attracting money into your life.

"I am so happy and grateful now that money comes to me in increasing quantities through multiple sources on a continuous basis."

If possible, verbally state your affirmations out loud several times every day. If you are unable to say them out loud, then say them within your mind. Allow yourself to center your entire focus and attention on reciting these statements without any distractions.

The 20 Million Dollar Ticket

How much money are you currently making? How much money do you think that you should be making? A large number of people feel that they are only entitled to make up to a certain amount of money each year. This type of thinking is referred to as a "self-limiting belief."

Think about this for a moment. If you were given a twenty million dollar lottery ticket, would you accept it? More than likely you would take the ticket and then run over to the lottery office to get the money. Why? This is perceived to be a lot of money and it could enhance the quality of your life. However, a number of people restrict themselves when it comes to how much money they should make. This is just a matter of perception. Maybe you have been conditioned to believe that you should only make a certain salary. However, if given the opportunity to have a twenty million dollar lottery ticket, you would cash it and not think twice about it. You may have been raised with a limited belief that you should go to work every day and just make a set salary. If this is your thought process, it needs to be changed.

There are a number of people who won millions of dollars in the lottery and end up losing the entire amount. Why? This may go back to their subconscious conditioning in which they feel they are not worthy to have that much money. Whatever you hold within your mind will be manifested in an outward manner. They may have lost the money because they felt that they didn't deserve it.

First, you must release the self-limiting beliefs that you are holding onto at a conscious and subconscious level. Second, you must believe that you deserve to have unlimited riches. After this is achieved, you will be open and receptive to receiving an abundance of wealth. Simply stated, your mindset shapes your destiny and future.

Millionaire System for Developing a Mindset for Success

1. Celebrate life with energy and enthusiasm; live your passion.
2. Develop a prosperity consciousness.
3. Accelerate your intellectual growth toward a higher level.

"I learned that when we crash into death's doorstep, we're all forced to ask three questions: Did I live? Did I love? Did I matter? It was a soul-shaking experience, to say the least, and it made me question everything in my life. I had never really lived before, and the accident made me get serious about doing so."

—Brendon Burchard
The Charge: Activating the 10 Human Drives That Make You Feel Alive

1. Celebrate life with energy and enthusiasm; live your passion

Several years ago, Brendon Burchard was involved in a very serious car accident. Being thrown into a potentially life-threatening event was the catalyst that elevated Brendon to a greater emotional awakening. "There's a sense of aliveness, there's a sense of energy, and enthusiasm engaging with the moment that really makes me feel that charge," said Brendon. As a result, he is able to live passionately every day.

All the millionaires in this book love life and have a very positive attitude that transmits energy and enthusiasm. They are living their passion and doing what they love on a daily basis. In addition, they are providing great products, services, courses, seminars, and coaching to their clients and customers. Their energy level is so high that it can't be repressed. This energetic vibrational force is flowing out to the world and then coming back to them.

When you look deep inside your heart and soul, you will discover your purpose. When you are able to combine this love with a deep care and concern for others, you will be able to reach your dreams.

Years ago, it was acceptable to follow a secure path in life. Your grandparents, parents, and teachers may have suggested that you pursue a career path that was safe. In today's society, the old school approach and mentality doesn't work anymore. There are countless well-established companies that have either gone bankrupt or completely shut down. As a result, employees find themselves out of work. A company cannot guarantee your job security; you guarantee your own security by developing a skill that can help others. By sharing your expertise, you will find that your talents are in high demand and this will bring in a consistent source of customers, clients, and income. Realize that people who are prosperous usually have multiple streams of income and this opens the door for unlimited opportunities.

It is not being recommended that you leave your current job. We all have to survive, pay our bills, and provide for our families. However, if you hold a passion for another career, you can start the training that you need in order to get there. You can stay with your job until you are able to obtain a profession that you really love and then you can transfer into your new occupation. A number of people have a dream of becoming an entrepreneur. Maybe you would like to become a speaker, coach, or consultant. What is your dream? What career would you love? If you can't answer these questions now, that's ok. Meditate on your true passion but don't procrastinate too long with making a decision.

A lot of people are just going through the motion of their daily activities without any feeling or passion. They are like robots and lack any type of emotion or feeling. When you talk to them, their voice is monotone and there is no energy. As a result, your first inclination is to push away from them and find someone who is more upbeat, positive, and flowing with enthusiasm.

Some people will push their dreams into the future but they never take the steps in order to reach them. They will always find an excuse for not working on their goals. They might say the following:

- I will work on my ambitions after I get my degree…
- I will start my own business when I have more money…
- I will begin my speaking career after I get more certifications…
- I will wait until the economy gets better before I become an entrepreneur…

When someone makes excuses for not working on their aspirations, they will never achieve them. However, people who succeed find innovative and creative ways to accomplish their hopes and desires.

Imagine for a moment. You just discovered that you won millions of dollars in the lottery. Can you begin to realize your level of excitement and happiness? This would be dramatic and everyone around you would feel your energy level. You would have a challenging time trying to restrain your emotions. At that moment, nothing would stop you from going down to the lottery office and cashing in your winning ticket. Think about this. How about taking that same level of enthusiasm and transferring it over to a dream that you really want to achieve? Why just allow yourself to get excited over winning the lottery? If you incorporate the eight success strategies into your daily routine, you will attain financial and emotional abundance. You can have the life of your dreams but you must be willing to take action.

There is another critical element for your success. You will discover that when you are concerned about helping other people, you will be propelled to a higher emotional level. Understand that there needs to be a genuine concern for helping others rather than an obsession with getting rich. When you are able to accomplish this, wealth will automatically flow to you.

Realize that your energy and enthusiasm level will also be significantly enhanced when you have gratitude.

As a part of your daily reflection and mediation:

- Have gratitude for all of your current blessings.
- Be thankful for all of the blessings that you are going to receive in the future.

2. Develop a prosperity consciousness

Bob Proctor noted in his book, *You Were Born Rich,* "One of the reasons that wealthy people have money is that they have developed the state of consciousness we will hereinafter refer to as, a 'prosperity consciousness.' If we wish to attract money to ourselves, we must begin to foster a prosperity consciousness as well." In order to accomplish this, it is important to see yourself already in possession of the amount of money that you desire.

Proctor said that you need to have a mindset for productivity and growth. It is imperative to always go after a higher level. Bob further stated that we've got to learn the laws of wealth. Simply put, if you have the appropriate thoughts regarding the acquisition of money, you will begin to attract it into your life. However, understand that wealth needs to be acquired honestly and then it will keep growing.

According to James Malinchak, there is a poverty way of thinking and a prosperity way of thinking. To illustrate this point, James told a story about someone spending ten dollars on a book. If the person starts to complain about spending the money, they are coming from a poverty way of thinking. However, if the person believes they just made an investment in their future success, they are utilizing a prosperity way of thinking. James also stated that a person needs to develop the necessary skills in a particular area to be successful. Lastly, taking action is also required.

As outlined by Malinchak, you need to:

1. Develop the right mindset.
2. Get the appropriate skillset.
3. Take the required action.

You will attract into your life either a positive or negative energy depending upon whatever you focus your thoughts on. If you have a negative mindset regarding the acquisition of money, you need to discard this immediately. With wealth comes the ability to expand, grow, and help others.

3. Accelerate your intellectual growth toward a higher level

There is a natural desire to keep growing, expanding, and learning on this life journey. Through continuing education, you permit yourself to increase your intellectual capabilities. It is a matter of becoming actively involved with reading books, investing in home study courses, attending seminars, working with an accountability partner, seeking out a mentor, and becoming involved with master mind groups.

The most successful people are always trying to challenge themselves by attaining a higher goal. For example, Sean D. Tucker achieved excellence and recognition for being a phenomenal aerobatic pilot but he does not stop there. He is constantly working on his aerobatic routines in order to execute them with complete precision, accuracy, and safety. When Sean is not flying, he is challenging himself by attempting to master the skill of mountain climbing.

It is important to set ambitions that you want to achieve. When you reach a particular goal, work on another dream that you want to attain. Keep in mind that you need to keep your aspirations within a reasonable number so that you don't become overwhelmed. Sometimes starting off with a smaller list is better than coming up with a bigger list that might have a tendency to overwhelm you. Write down your dreams and when you reach them, check them off. At this point, you will feel triumphant and then you can start working on your next set of goals.

When you examine people who have retired, you will discover that a number of them have lost their purpose and excitement. They stopped living. We all need to strive for more. People who retired and took on other responsibilities, careers, hobbies, and challenges continue to thrive in life. As a result, their growth continues in an upward direction regardless of age.

Lessons Learned

"The millionaire mindset simply says, 'I don't care what you throw at me today; I will overcome and will do better than I did yesterday.' There are going to be challenges. You expect the challenge and you're excited to take on the day and become a winner. I believe we are positive people. We wake up knowing we're going to have success and nothing can stop us. We might fail and we'll pick ourselves up, dust ourselves off, and go at it again the next day. Then, we have success and don't have to pep ourselves up. The success that you have gives you the mindset for the next day and that mindset creates success. It makes you wake up feeling great knowing you can do it again. The success that you have fuels your mindset; your mindset fuels your success."

—**Mike Filsaime**

Realize this. If you are just obsessed with making money, it may come to you temporarily but it won't last. However, if you are genuinely concerned about providing great value to other people and helping them, you will become prosperous. The highlighted millionaires in this book started their business because they wanted to make a real difference and serve other people. Through their products, services, coaching, and seminars, they are helping others on a consistent basis with a genuine concern. As a result, they are blessed with an abundance of wealth.

Your mindset is critical to your victory. When you maintain the right attitude, it doesn't matter what obstacle is thrown into your path; you will find a way to get through it or you will find an innovative way to go around it. Nothing will stop you from achieving what you want.

Permit yourself to become focused on what you want to achieve. You must believe in yourself and what you are capable of accomplishing even if you don't feel it one hundred percent right now. Start believing that you can attain whatever you want and don't give up on yourself. It doesn't matter what anyone else may have told you. You will definitely reach whatever you focus on if you are committed and take decisive action. Allow yourself to embrace the setbacks you encounter as a valuable learning experience and recognize that they are only temporary.

Don't allow your emotional growth to stop; if it does, your enthusiasm for life will diminish greatly. When we are striving for our goals and taking action toward reaching them, we project a positive energy that can be felt by others who are around us. If you give up because things aren't going your way, your enthusiasm and passion will disappear.

You must take action! This is what prosperous people do. However, when you are doing something that you absolutely love, you won't view it as work. The millionaires are doing what they love; it is their passion. This is their driving force that gets them up in the morning and provides them with the energy to keep moving ahead.

A large number of individuals have given up on their dreams. They have decided to just settle for what they currently have. Subsequently, they have become very robotic in their daily activities and have no passion for living. Life is meant to be lived fully with enthusiasm.

If you don't pursue your dreams and goals, what is the alternative? You can stay at home and spend countless hours on the coach or in bed. Over time, your energy level will gradually decrease. You will never feel fulfilled and you will miss the happiness and joy from living a passionate life. Later, when you look back on what you could have accomplished, you will have massive regret because you gave up pursuing your ambitions. From this moment forward, the choices that you make will shape your destiny. You can either remain complacent or get active.

Don't make excuses! Don't procrastinate! Don't push off taking action until next week or next month! The excuses must stop and you must get active. Even though you may have a busy schedule, become creative, develop effective time management skills, work on high-priority tasks, and take the steps to achieve your aspirations.

Master Mind Action Steps:

Action Step #1: Make a list of your dreams and goals that you feel passionate about. After your list is completed, place the most important goal in position number one and go down from there. Decide what steps you are going to take in order to accomplish each item on your list. After that, get a calendar and write down estimated completion dates for each action step under the goals. When they are completed, check them off.

Action Step #2: Start thinking, feeling, and acting as if you have an abundance of wealth and happiness right now in your life. Develop affirmations that are related to reaching your aspirations. Get a dream board. On your board, outline all of your dreams and goals with pictures and words.

Action Step #3: Do your homework. Find books, home study courses, seminars, accountability partners, mentors, and master mind groups that will help you and provide you with the necessary resources to reach all of your dreams and goals.

> *"You'll never shift your mindset. More importantly, you will never shift your spirit and you will never take action as long as you're allowing people to pollute you. You got to stop listening to the garbage, what I call the N-I-O-P-S, the Negative Influence of Other People, cause they'll derail you. When they pollute your mind, it pollutes your heart, your spirit. It immobilizes you. It's like throwing you in park. It's like paralyzing you, putting handcuffs on you, and there is no way you'll take action as long as you're listening to that garbage."*

> **—James Malinchak**

Chapter 7
GENEROSITY AND GRATITUDE

"Gratitude is essential. Gratitude hooks you up with your source of supply. We have so much to be grateful for. The more grateful you are, the more good you will attract. Giving is absolutely essential. The more you give, the more you receive. You don't give to receive, you give to give. You give the energy and you have more come to you. It's a law. You're merely a distributor."

—Bob Proctor

W hen you analyze all of the millionaire success strategies, it is imperative to focus on the concept of generosity and gratitude. These are vital principles that must become part of your life and they will help to ensure your success. By giving to others with a genuine "pureness of heart" and without any expectation of receiving anything back in return, you are allowing positive energy to flow into your life. Also, by developing a mindset of gratitude, you are enabling yourself to receive a greater abundance of financial and emotional wealth.

Generosity is rarely mentioned when people talk about millionaires. There seems to be a tendency to focus only on the amount of money that someone may have. However, a large number of prosperous individuals are actively donating their money to churches and worthwhile causes on a continuous basis. Often, these acts of kindness are done quietly and without any media attention. As a result, the general public is usually unaware of the true expression of thoughtfulness that is being extended to others by these affluent individuals.

When James Malinchak appeared on ABC's "*Secret Millionaire*" television show, he gave away over $100,000 of his own money. He is committed to giving back to others. "I know personally how much money, how much time, how much talent, how much skills I'm giving away every year to those less fortunate. It's just a great way to be, great way to live, and I think everybody should do it. As a matter of fact, in my Big Money Speaker Boot Camp, we've raised in the last few years $600,000 just from all audience members there to help kids because I have a special place in my heart for kids. I always start off usually with a ten thousand dollar check because I just want to start the giving.... it's great to have a seminar that makes money but I want us to be giving back as a community as well and helping the less fortunate. It's just something that's important to me and I've been so blessed because of that," said James.

Sean D. Tucker is someone who extends generosity to others from his heart. He was named Chairman of the EAA Young Eagles program which is based in Oshkosh, Wisconsin. He volunteers his time and energy to an organization focused on introducing young boys and girls between the ages of 8 and 17 to the world of aviation. Volunteer pilots from the Experimental Aircraft Association (EAA) offer their time and planes to give introductory flights to children and teens. As Chairman,

Tucker is responsible for leading the Young Eagles program in a positive direction forward while encouraging more young people to become involved within the field of aviation.

Sean's commitment to serving others has also extended to another area. He founded a non-profit organization which is called "Every Kid Can Fly" which helps disadvantaged teens by teaching them how to solo an aircraft on their own. By accomplishing this objective, the teens are able to develop a level of self-esteem and self-confidence which may have been lacking from their life. The goal of this program is to change their perception of what they are truly capable of achieving. Every Kid Can Fly teaches teens about the science of aviation and takes them off the street and puts them into the cockpit of an airplane.

As Chairman of the Young Eagles Program and founder of Every Kid Can Fly, Tucker shares his time, talent, and experience with children. This reflects Sean's genuine concern that he has for other people.

Let's take a look at Anthony Robbins. He is a respected entrepreneur, author, and peak performance strategist. He gained a very positive reputation for helping countless people through his books, products, courses, and seminars. Several years ago, Robbins founded an organization called The International Basket Brigade which "is built on a simple notion; one small act of generosity on the part of one caring person can transform the lives of hundreds." Volunteers will prepare a basket of food, clothing, or household items and personally deliver it to a needy family or individual. This charitable organization is responsible for helping an estimated two million people annually in countries all over the world.

If you share and give to others, the level of energy that you receive back will produce tremendous results. At this point, you will discover that your motivation to pursue your objectives will be intensified and you will be focused on obtaining your dreams.

The Challenge

"The more you give, the more it comes back to you."
—Russell Brunson

It is acceptable to desire substantial wealth but this can't be your primary concentration. Your life journey needs to be focused on giving to others. When this level is achieved, positive energy will be transferred back to you in monumental proportion. Subsequently, you will be rewarded with prosperity.

You might believe that millionaires are constantly consumed with the idea of making money. This is a misconception. In reality, their attention is centered on giving to others. They are able to appreciate the fact that money will accumulate on a continual basis as long as they are assisting other people. As a result, they are dedicated to providing products, courses, seminars, and coaching programs that make the world a better place.

When the concept of generosity is discussed, there might be an inclination to do it for self-centered reasons. Comprehend the fact that there is a definite rhythm to the laws of the universe. As such, you can either work in harmony with the universe or you can work against it. Permit yourself to reach deep inside your soul and make the conscious decision to help others with a genuine concern. If you are motivated by selfish reasons, wealth may be acquired but it won't grow or last. Someone who cares only about themselves will break the cycle of generosity. When this happens, the natural law of reciprocity will not occur. Simply stated, develop sincere motives for your actions.

There are countless examples of well-known individuals who lost their fortune when they became selfish and disregarded other people. At that point, a number of them became consumed with alcoholism or drug abuse because they were searching for that magic pill that would bring them inner peace and happiness. They thought that money alone would give them total joy but they were wrong. Money can enhance your life when you are giving fully to others but a substantial bank account doesn't have any meaning if greed is allowed to consume your purpose for living. Understand that true happiness and inner peace comes from sharing kindness and love with other people.

Realize that prosperous individuals are actively involved in tithing whereby they will donate at least ten percent of their income to a church, charitable organization, or to someone in financial need. In the book, *The Miracle of Tithing,* Mark Victor Hansen wrote, "Tithing is the best kept prosperity secret in existence... Tithing works because it works from inside you. It changes your belief that life is about taking, to a new understanding that life is about giving. Giving guarantees receiving. It always has and it always will. What is amazing is that giving expands your spirituality, especially when you give in the spirit of love, joy, and cheerfulness from an unselfish heart."

Another important element of your framework for success needs to be focused on being thankful for what you currently have and for what you will receive in the future. After careful analysis of the millionaires highlighted in this book, it is evident that they incorporate a feeling of gratitude throughout their entire life, both professionally and personally. When you are truly able to appreciate the blessings that you have on a daily basis, you are opening yourself up to receiving more.

Millionaire System for Having Generosity and Gratitude

1. Give with a pureness of heart and have gratitude.
2. Perform "three small acts of kindness."
3. Create high quality products, services, and coaching programs.

"When you give and you're generous, then things just happen for you when you do it just to do it because it's the right thing to do. When you're generous with your life, God is generous in your life."

—**James Malinchak**

1. Give with a pureness of heart and have gratitude

There is a critical point that needs to be understood. When you give to someone else, it must be done with a "pureness of heart" and you can't have any expectation of getting anything back in return. If you are only giving to receive something back, you will not receive anything. However, if you are truly giving with a genuine kindness, it will return to you in many positive ways. Simply stated, you are meant to share with an open heart. By giving, you are sending out a ripple effect of love to the world and this will return to you as long as your intentions are pure and honest.

There are basic laws that govern the universe. When you are able to appreciate the concept of sharing and giving to other people, you will be blessed financially and emotionally. If you are only concerned about making money and holding onto every single dollar, you might get rich in the short term but it will not last. In time, the money will disappear.

Think about this for a moment. What happens when you give a gift to a friend or family member? Do you expect anything from them? Most likely, you are giving to them because of unconditional love and you don't want anything back. This is the purest form of giving and the positive energy transmitted with this act of love is tremendous.

There is a well-guarded secret that is known within the inner circle of millionaires. They recognize the great importance of giving to other people without any anticipation of receiving anything in return. Realize that the money you acquire is a reflection of your generosity and from the service you provide to others.

In addition to sharing, you also need to surround yourself with gratitude. On a daily basis, be appreciative for the blessings which you currently have and be thankful for what you are going to receive in the future.

2. Perform "three small acts of kindness"

Starting today, think of three people and do a small act of kindness for each one of them during this next week. It can be a neighbor, co-worker, distant relative, or even a stranger. The key point is to do a small act of kindness that you wouldn't normally do for each one of these three people. It could be as simple as going to the store for them, bringing them lunch or dinner, giving them a small gift, or visiting with them. You will put a smile on their face and they will know that someone cares about them.

By engaging in the above exercise on a weekly basis, you are helping people and this energetic vibrational wave will be sent out the universe and you will receive it back. As time goes on, you will become elevated to a higher level of emotional awareness. After you become actively involved in doing three small acts of kindness on a consistent basis, the positive rewards that will flow into your life both financially and emotionally will be significant.

In addition to becoming actively involved with three small acts of kindness, you can also make financial contributions to a church, charitable organization, or person in need. Mark Victor Hansen makes this recommendation, "If you read *One Minute Millionaire*, it says: give ten, save ten, invest ten, and live on seventy percent of your income." This simple formula for giving, saving, and investing money from Hansen is a great method for organizing your finances.

When you begin to study affluent people, you will discover that they donate large amounts of money to charities that they feel passionate about. When they allow their kindness and love to flow outward to other people, this energy comes back to them. However, any charitable act that is done for selfish goals will generate the opposite result. Extend charity to others with the right intention.

3. Create high quality products, services, and coaching programs

When you want to become financially independent, it is important to create high quality products and services that solve a problem. When you are able to provide products, courses, coaching, and seminars that genuinely benefit others, you are ensuring your victory.

When entrepreneurs become focused only on making money, the quality of their products and services are diminished. Openly share your knowledge with your customers and clients. The most important goal is to provide high quality goods and services. Then, revenue and profits will come as a result.

Lessons Learned

"Generosity and giving back is a universal law. It's the law of the universe; what you put out there will come back to you. In this expanding universe, everything is always going to be bigger than when it started. So, you cannot give only because you know it's going to come back to you greater. Then, you're violating that rule because you are doing it for yourself and that's not the point. You have to give with no expectation of receiving in return… You want to have some type of philanthropy in your life where you can take what God or the universe has given you and share it with others. It is definitely important to give back to charities, foundations, and the less fortunate."

—Mike Filsaime

Generosity and gratitude are essential to your ultimate success. When you are able to welcome these two elements into your daily routine, you will attract an abundance of financial and emotional wealth into your life. You must have genuine motives when you are extending kindness to other people.

Understand that when you send out positive energy to the universe, you will receive it back. Likewise, if you send out negative energy to the universe, you will receive undesirable results. So, it is important to completely remove any feelings of selfishness and replace that with sharing and giving. When you are able to accomplish this, your results will be amazing.

It is simply a matter of modeling after the highly successful millionaires presented in this book. If you follow their same framework, you can attain substantial results.

Four Types of Generosity:

There are four types of generosity that can be easily integrated into your life:

1. Make a financial donation to a charitable organization, church, or individual in need.
2. Donate your time, effort, and energy to a worthy cause or non-profit organization.
3. Engage in "Three Small Acts of Kindness" on a continuous basis in which you extend kindness and sharing to a minimum of three people.
4. Share your knowledge with others for free.

It is also imperative that you spend quality time with your spouse, children, family, and friends. Time has a tendency to pass by very quickly and it is easy to become consumed with our daily activities. We must challenge ourselves to avoid pushing people we care about to the side. When you are going to spend time with your family and friends, turn off the television, stop surfing the internet, stop sending text messages, and just focus your entire attention on the person that you love and care about. This is one of the greatest gifts that you can give to someone who means the world to you.

If you are only consumed with getting rich, you will not be successful. Focus your attention on assisting other people and making their life better. If you are able to achieve this type of mindset, the money will flow in as a natural progression because your intentions are focused in the right direction. If you are trying to receive gratification from just making money, you will gain only short term satisfaction. However, if you can allow yourself to be motivated by a desire to be creative and assist others, the rewards you get will be tremendous.

When Russell Brunson conducted seminars, he could tell which people had a real purpose and wanted to make a true difference. Russell said that ninety percent of the people at his seminars were there because they just wanted to make money. For the remaining ten percent, their desire was to create value and change the world. He said that this group was always a success and the other ninety percent left the seminar and never did anything. When you provide value to other people, you will be successful.

Realize it is essential to be thankful for all of your blessings. You may not be at your ideal point in life in regards to your financial statement but you still have things that you can be grateful for. In addition, also appreciate the inner peace, happiness, contentment, and financial wealth that will come into your life. By having an appreciation for what you currently have and for what you will receive, you are opening the door to an abundance of positive energy.

Generosity and gratitude are essential elements that must be incorporated into your life on a daily basis.

Master Mind Action Steps

Action Step #1: Take a certain percentage of your income and donate or tithe it to a church, charitable organization, or person in need. As mentioned in this chapter, ten percent is suggested for tithing. If you are limited on financial resources, you can always give your time to an organization that you feel passionate about. When you are giving, ensure that you have the right intention and that you are not doing it for selfish reasons.

Action Step #2: At the beginning of each week, make a list of at least three people and write down one small act of kindness you are going to do for each one. You can put them on your calendar and check off each act of kindness after you complete it.

Action Step #3: Think of products, services, or a coaching program that can genuinely help other people. You may want to consider donating some of your time and sharing your expertise with other people within your industry without any expectation of receiving anything back.

"I can inspire people through flight, but am I every single day making the world a better place? Am I touching somebody in a positive way every single day? Am I doing my job as a human being to affect positive change in the world for goodness? That's how I measure success."

—**Sean D. Tucker**

Chapter 8
TAKING DECISIVE ACTION: MAGNETIC ACTION PRINCIPLE (MAP)

"With a limited amount of time on this planet, to just sit, and wait, and twirl our fingers, that's going to ultimately culminate into an unlived life. So, we have to choose what is important to us and we have to move swiftly towards it because the only other option is a life on the sidelines and that doesn't feel good because when you're just watching everyone else play the game of life, you're not enjoying it, and you're just sitting there as a spectator. At some point, you can only watch so many games before it's not fun anymore."

—Brendon Burchard

In addition to the seven success strategies outlined so far, there is an eighth strategy that is essential for your ultimate victory; taking decisive action. If you decide to sit back and become complacent, you will achieve absolutely nothing of significance or meaning within your life. Appreciate the fact that time continues to pass by every day and you have total choice in whether or not you are going to become an active participant.

Let's face it. Money is not going to drop out of the sky into your lap. It is very rare for anyone to win the lottery. However, if you are truly committed to reaching your goals through all obstacles, you will gain a tremendous amount of wealth, happiness, joy, and contentment.

If you don't take any action, your life will be unfulfilled because there was never any movement toward your ambitions and you will experience regret. Realize that you have the choice to shape your future and destiny in any manner that you want. Understand that your past is behind you and is history. Don't focus on the past; center your attention on what is ahead. Total control and power comes from your ability to shape your future in whatever direction you want. Stop making excuses for not moving forward.

It is easy to become consumed with our daily obligations and push things off to a later time or day. Also, if you allow procrastination, hesitation, indecisiveness, or a lack of motivation to prevent you from working on your aspirations, you will never obtain your inner desires. However, if you get up, get active, and start pushing toward your ambitions through all challenges with a determined attitude, you will succeed. Commit yourself to becoming fully engaged so that the life of your dreams can become a reality.

When you make a conscious and deliberate decision to begin your journey, you need to formulate a plan or framework for accomplishing your objectives. At this point, list the steps which are required to reach your goals. Devote your time to conducting research and reflecting upon the steps that will get you to your final destination. Without a plan, your chances of victory are diminished. After you complete each item on your list, be sure to place a check mark next to it.

If you really want to achieve your aspirations, you can always find innovative methods to ensure your success. For example, let's say your dream was to write a book. If you sat down and wrote just one page a day, you would have 180 pages written within six months. At that point, you could make your revisions and be ready to publish your book. If you stayed up an extra half hour at night and got up an extra half hour in the morning, then you would be devoting an hour a day to achieving your eventual dream of becoming an author. Can you imagine the results if you spent two hours a day working on productive activities directly related to what you want to accomplish?

Maybe you would like to leave your current job and follow your passion. However, before you make that leap, you would like to ensure that you will be making enough money to cover your bills and provide for your family. A large number of individuals will start working on their new career while they still have their current job. After they discover that the new position will generate a much larger income, they will leave their job and devote their attention to their new business.

Suppose your dream is to become a speaker and share your knowledge with others. If you average $5,000 per speech and get paid to do just two speeches per month, you will make $120,000 for the year. In order to become a speaker, you will have to reach out to event coordinators and let them know you are available to speak at their college, university, organization, or event. If you spend an hour or two a day just contacting event coordinators, do you think that you could get at least two speaking engagements per month? With just two speeches per month, you will make $120,000 for the entire year.

Let's say you want to host your own seminar or workshop. If you conduct four events per year and get twenty five students at each event, you only need to charge $1,000 tuition for each attendee in order to make $100,000 for the year. How would you like to share your expertise through coaching and consulting? If you are able to get only nine coaching clients and they pay you a $1,000 per month, you will make $108,000 for the year.

When you become creative, you will discover several areas for making a six or seven figure income per year. At the end of this book, there is a section called: "The Road to a Million Dollars: 10 Areas for Wealth Creation." In this section, you will find ten income opportunities that can generate substantial wealth.

Magnetic Action Principle – MAP

There is a clarification that needs to be made before you can advance onward. You need to discard any past negative conditioning or self-limiting beliefs that you may have. The ability to be open and receptive is a critical aspect for attaining ultimate victory.

Some people have a negative association regarding the concept of "work." Let's reshape your perception. Instead of focusing on "work", replace the word with "action." Realize that your thoughts are very powerful and can determine your energetic vibrational level. Now, center your attention on taking "action." This word has a positive association and should become part of your mindset. You get more accomplished when you are thinking about it as taking action instead of viewing it as work. Some might say this is just a play on words but it is more important than that. Your overall mental perception can shape your entire life.

Comprehend that when you choose a career path that you love, it won't be work to you. Your enthusiasm for doing what you love will launch you to a higher level of financial and emotional peace. Simply put, you can obtain any of your dreams.

After examining and analyzing all of the success strategies for the highlighted millionaires in this book, it was discovered that they utilize a very powerful principle. From this point forward, this will be referred to as the "Magnetic Action Principle" or MAP for short. The implementation of MAP allowed these affluent individuals to acquire substantial wealth, happiness, self-confidence, and inner peace. Their victory was a direct result of sending out a positive energy to the universe while simultaneously taking decisive action on a daily basis. At this point, a magnetic field was activated and riches were drawn to them. These two elements work together in complete harmony to produce astonishing results.

Magnetic Action Principle Formula:
Decisive & Consistent Action + Positive Vibrational Energy
= Dreams & Goals

Decisive and consistent action must be taken on a daily basis. Before you begin, take the time to do your research and write out the steps you will need in order to reach your final objectives.

Positive Vibrational Energy

Send out a positive energy to the universe and allow it to permeate throughout your entire mind, heart, and spirit. When you are fully able to understand the true power of this concept, you will receive whatever you want.

At some point in the past, maybe you had a high vibrational level toward reaching your ambitions but as time went on, this may have drifted away. It is time to revitalize that passion that you held within your heart and soul. Allow yourself to become excited again for what you truly want to attain and permit that desire to be the catalyst for propelling you forward to achieving your goals. Starting now, maintain a strong commitment to attaining all of your aspirations.

The secret ingredient that all of the millionaires have which make them highly successful and unstoppable is their rock solid faith that they will succeed. At times they may fail but they quickly brush off these momentary setbacks and keep pushing ahead with a determined confidence. With a strong self-confidence, they are able to transmit immense positive energy out to the universe. If you are able to incorporate this same type of mindset into your daily routine, you will become elevated to the same vibrational wavelength as the millionaires presented within the pages of this book.

In a manner of speaking, you are traveling at a high rate of speed to your destination. At this point, nothing will stop your momentum onward unless you make the decision to derail yourself and then you will go off the tracks ending your progression forward. Contrary to what some people believe, the only person that can stop you from achieving all of your dreams and goals is you. Those around you may say hurtful things to you. You may fail over and over again. However, if you are dedicated to reaching your aspirations, you will achieve victory.

Have you ever noticed that some people seem to keep getting things handed to them over and over again? On the surface, it would appear that they have very good luck. But it is not a matter of just good luck or having a four leaf clover in their purse or wallet. In reality, they are transmitting energy out to the universe and it is coming back to them.

At times, you may receive advice from family and friends regarding your dreams which may be somewhat negative thereby minimizing your level of excitement. Some people are very quick to offer their suggestions. When someone else expresses their opinion regarding your dream or goal, they are giving a recommendation based upon their own limited feelings. They might have the best intention but unable to consider your dream objectively and they give advice from their own prejudices or feelings. What is right for them may not be right for you. However, don't automatically reject all ideas. Examine it carefully and objectively analyze the entire situation. Then, you can choose the best path that will get you to your objectives.

To summarize MAP, it is imperative that you begin to take decisive and consistent action while maintaining a positive vibrational energy that radiates throughout your body and is transmitted out to the world. Action is critical for your momentum forward and this will guarantee substantial results.

Realize that you must have an ultimate goal in mind and a general blueprint. Take some time and think about a detailed plan for what you really want to achieve and what steps are needed to get you there. If you drive your car to an unknown location, you need a map or GPS to help you arrive at your destination. Likewise, it is important to have a mind map so that you can reach your aspirations.

The Challenge

"Decisive action is absolutely essential... You've got to move into action. You got to get out there and do it. Don't just talk about it, you've got to do it... Make decisions fast. Follow your intuition. Follow the quiet voice within. It's telling you the way to go."
—Bob Proctor

If you are totally committed and become active, you are going to attain whatever you want. However, if you are unwilling to move ahead, then you will never achieve your inner desires. Understand that winners fail over and over again but they consistently keep advancing toward their ambitions. They don't allow themselves to get consumed with failures and setbacks. Rather, they keep focused on their eventual objective with an unwavering commitment to being successful. Simply put, taking decisive action on a consistent basis will allow you to receive an abundance of financial and emotional wealth.

Your conscious decision to move ahead must be made with a hundred percent commitment. Think through your options. As time passes by, do you want to be an active participant or someone who just sits on the couch and becomes complacent? As humans, we all have an internal desire to keep growing and learning. If you permit yourself to stay on the sidelines and watch life pass by, you will be lacking joy, happiness, and inner peace because you are not living up to your fullest potential. As time passes, regret will become prominent and the "I don't care" attitude will become your primary focus. Don't allow yourself to fall into this trap. Get busy starting today and be open and receptive to taking the steps in order to accomplish your dreams.

At times, we become trapped within our own protective bubble and we "just settle" in life. At that point, we are consumed by indifference and there is no desire to reach any dream or goal. This false sense of security gives us an unrealistic view of the true reality. None of the millionaires in this book will allow themselves to "just settle" and they excel above and beyond to create the life of their dreams. You have received enlightenment from this book and you can't make any more excuses for not taking action. Your protective bubble has been popped and it is time to start living fully and vibrantly. You will be blessed with an abundance of wealth, joy, happiness, and inner peace if you are open and receptive to start pushing ahead.

It is time to throw your excuses out the window. Just take a look at any actor, actress, professional athlete, or musical artist who reached the top of their profession. They were able to obtain their ultimate dream with a determined mindset. Shift your mind in a different direction and focus on being totally active.

Millionaire System for Taking Decisive Action

1. Develop an effective time management plan.
2. Research options and make decisions quickly.
3. Take decisive action.

"A great way to take action is to find people who are already doing what you want to do. Go near them, learn from them, let them inspire you because they're playing at a higher level and just by seeing them and watching them, and what they do, and the action they take, it automatically pulls you up just by watching them and listening to them."

—**James Malinchak**

1. Develop an effective time management plan

Utilizing effective time management strategies is probably the most challenging obstacle that you need to master in order to attain all of your aspirations. It is possible to balance your current job and family obligations while working toward your new career and goals. Once you become skillful at mastering your time, the possibilities for your eventual success will be unlimited.

Through the use of time management skills, there is always a way to find time to work on what you want to achieve. Several years ago, there was a woman who got married very young and had several children. However, she had a major dream. She wanted to go back to school and get her master's degree so that she could teach. But, she was living day-to-day just surviving. From the moment she woke up in the morning, she was busy with work, the children, and family obligations. Nonetheless, she made it a priority to go back to school. When her children went to bed at night, she would stay up for an extra hour or two so that she could do homework even though she was very tired. In spite of the challenge, she persisted. In the end, she received her degree and became a professor at DePaul University in Chicago.

There is a key point to keep in mind. Time is going to pass by at the same rate whether you are watching television for hours, lying in bed sleeping the day away, or going out and actively taking steps toward achieving your dreams. You can either make excuses for not taking action or you can find time to start working on your objectives. If you are able to organize your schedule every day to work on projects that will bring you closer to your aspirations, you will be amazed at the end of the month what you have completed.

Time management skills are not usually taught in school and it is very easy to become consumed with activities that don't accomplish anything of significance. At times, it might be nice to enjoy a favorite television show or surf the internet. However, you need to become laser focused on what you really want to achieve and take the steps that are going to eventually get you to your dreams.

Some people will find excuses and say that they just don't have the time to work on their ambitions because they are too busy. This is an example of the postponement strategy. They want to keep pushing off taking action. As a result, they will never attain their goals.

Let's take a look at effective time management skills which can be implemented starting today.

Effective Time Management Steps

1. Organize your mandatory daily activities hour-by-hour on a calendar. This may include working your current job, taking your children to school, or completing a required errand.

2. As you organize your daily activities, set aside quality time for your spouse, partner, and children.

3. Limit your recreation time to only one hour per day. This may include watching television, responding to email, surfing the internet, or sending text messages.

4. On your daily calendar, schedule time for working on high-priority tasks related to achieving your business and personal objectives.

5. Utilize idle time for productive activities. When you are traveling in your vehicle, turn off your radio and listen to an

audio book or seminar that is related to the dreams you want to attain. Also, when you are shopping or exercising, listen to a motivational seminar or home study course.

Let's assume that you spend a half hour in the morning when you wake up and a half hour at night before you go to bed working on tasks that will get you closer to reaching your goals. At the end of the month, you would have spent thirty hours being productive and advancing closer to your aspirations. It is simply a matter of turning off the television, stop surfing the internet for hours, stop sending continuous text messages, and start working on your ambitions.

You will find the time to work on your goals if you permit yourself to become creative. Focus your attention on tasks that have a high-priority so that you can advance closer to your aspirations. If you organize the hours throughout the day, time can be used wisely in an effective manner. Most people waste countless hours in the car listening to radio stations. This time can be spent learning and growing by listening to audio books and home study courses. If you spend at least an hour or two shopping, take your iPod, cell phone, or mp3 player with you and listen to something that will help you reach your ambitions. Also, think about activities that will help you attain your objectives. For example, you might need to read books within the area that you want to specialize in, take a home study course, attend seminars, become a member of a master mind group, and choose a mentor who can help you.

2. Research options and make decisions quickly

Whatever decision you decide to make, do your homework and make an informed choice based upon the facts. However, do not allow the excuse of conducting research to stop you from making a required decision. Your research should be done efficiently and a final choice should be made without delay. There have been a lot of great deals lost because of procrastination or hesitation.

In some cases, you may not have the time to do research. In these rare cases, you will have to make a decision based upon your experience and your feelings. Sometimes, our best choices are made quickly and based upon the intuition we feel. In those situations, trust yourself. Most likely, your internal instinct will be guiding you in the right direction. If a deal doesn't feel right for whatever reason, then take a pass. If you can, contact a trusted adviser or business associate and ask them for their suggestions and ideas.

Through indecisiveness and procrastination, you might miss out on an amazing life-altering opportunity. It is not being suggested that you make a determination in haste or without any careful thought or consideration. Just realize that successful people usually make a decision in an efficient manner after they have been presented with all the facts.

As stated by Mike Filsaime, the following four steps can be utilized when action needs to be taken:

1. Gather all the information that you can to make an informed decision.
2. Make the decision quick.
3. Stand by your decision based on the facts and the evidence.
4. Take decisive action as if your life depends on it.

3. Take decisive action

It doesn't matter where you are right now because you are embarking on a dramatic change for yourself and your business. Any negative internal scripts or attitudes have to be thrown out the window. You may have some fear because you are unsure of the future but you can't let this hold you back.

Young children learning a new task have no comprehension of "giving up" or just laying back and doing nothing. They are focused on obtaining their goal. As we get older, it seems that doubt and insecurity can sometimes prevent us from jumping ahead.

Your goals and dreams should be written down on a piece of paper and posted in a prominent location so that you can see them every day. Spend some time making a dream board and let it remind you constantly of what you are reaching for. There is a strong psychological element to utilizing this effective technique for shaping your future.

We all have an action altitude gauge that will determine the height to which we are going to soar in life and climb to success. As you complete high-priority tasks related to your objectives, your altitude will become higher and your confidence will begin to rise. The eventual goal is to reach the highest level possible and achieve all of your aspirations.

Don't waste time making excuses for inactivity; become focused on taking the necessary steps to obtain your goals.

Lessons Learned

"When you need to get something done, you're going to do it. You're not going to find time to make excuses. That's called being decisive because you know the consequences of inactivity and the great reward of taking action. Then, let's go for it. When we go to an extreme to get it done, we eliminate the self-limiting belief. When we make excuses and say, 'I don't know where to begin,' that's just an excuse. That's not being decisive. That's finding reasons to fail and an entrepreneur with a millionaire mindset simply says, 'There's a way to do this.' There is either 'I did it' or 'I didn't do it.' There is no such thing as saying 'I tried.' Just get it done."

—Mike Filsaime

The only way that you are going to accomplish anything of value is to get active. Anyone that tells you there is a push button for success is lying to you. When you have a desire that you want to achieve, you are going to have to work for it.

All of the millionaires highlighted within this book were not born into wealth. They had to work for their prosperity. For example:

- Bob Proctor was a high school dropout and started cleaning offices. He discovered a book from Napoleon Hill, *Think and Grow Rich*, that greatly affected his life. In time, he became a self-made millionaire.
- Brendon Burchard survived a car accident and persisted to become a highly respected motivational speaker and high performance trainer.
- Mark Victor Hansen was rejected by over a 140 publishers before he found a company that agreed to publish *Chicken Soup for the Soul*.
- Sean D. Tucker had to overcome a fear of flying before he could become a highly respected aerobatic pilot.
- James Malinchak didn't have any money but he would sit in the Barnes and Noble store and read every sales book that he could. When he did a product offering and nobody bought from him, he learned how to do presentations the right way.
- Russell Brunson tried to make money and he wasn't able to do it until he created his own product. He started his first online business as a college student and made a million dollars within a year of graduation.
- Steve Harrison was on the verge of bankruptcy until he discovered how to market his services in the correct manner.
- Mike Filsaime was working in the auto sales industry and read a report from John Reese which greatly impacted his

life. He launched Butterfly Marketing and did a million dollars in five days.

Through dedication, persistence, and action, the above millionaires achieved their dreams and goals. They did not sit on the sidelines and watch life pass them by. To the contrary, they became active participants on their life journey.

Here is the formula utilized by all successful millionaires:

Follow your passion by taking decisive action +
Provide great value with a genuine concern to help
people = Financial and emotional abundance

Think about this for a moment. There are countless examples of actors, athletes, musical artists, and business professionals who encountered numerous rejections and obstacles but continued to persist. Understand that anyone at the top of their profession had to work for that honor. However, after reaching success, the inner satisfaction and self-confidence that they feel is tremendous.

The path to your goals will involve work and setbacks will be encountered along the way. However, the reward for attaining your final dream will be huge. You have the power deep inside to shape your destiny in whatever manner you want. You can sit back and let life pass you by or you can make the decision right now to become an active participant.

It is time to throw any self-limiting beliefs out the window. Release any negative comments from other people regarding your talents or abilities. Whatever has happened in the past is gone forever. The past can only hold you back if you obsess over it. Focus on reaching your objectives. If you are truly committed to taking action, you will be rewarded and receive tremendous results.

Mastermind Action Steps:

Action Step #1: Developing effective time management is critical for reaching any of your ultimate objectives. Get a calendar where you can organize your daily routines on an hourly basis and include the following:

- Write down all of your activities that must be completed next to each hour.
- Spend time with your spouse, children, and family.
- Schedule time to work on high-priority tasks related to achieving your dreams.

Action Step #2: When presented with an important decision, do your homework and get busy researching your options so that you can make an informed choice. On a piece of paper, write down the results of your research and then analyze them so that you can make a wise decision. Sometimes, you may have to make a quick decision and then you will have to make that choice based upon your experience and inner feeling.

Action Step #3: Get ready for decisive action. After your research is completed and you can make an informed decision, don't second guess your choice. If you are working toward your dreams and goals, get out there and start doing the necessary steps that will get you closer to your aspirations. Make up a list of the steps that need to be completed and then check each one off as you finish them.

"I make decisions very quickly... you got to get good at making decisions and you got to realize that these decisions are coming all the time."

—Russell Brunson

Chapter 9

KEY ELEMENTS FOR EMPLOYEE MOTIVATION

"I demand from my employees that they take leadership. I demand from my employees that they have respect. I demand that I lead by example. I am the workplace spiritual advisor. I have to be ethical. I have to come in every day with it being a good day. I make the decision because if I come in and I'm having a bad day, they have a bad day; because they're looking to me as the leader to allow them to be successful and so I lead by example. If my employees don't take ownership of any part of my business, they know that they shouldn't be my employee because they're not on the team. They go above and beyond."

—Sean D. Tucker

There are several opinions regarding employee motivation. Some people believe a boss should just give out orders and it is the duty of an employee to obey. On the other hand, there are a considerable amount of managers, entrepreneurs, and business owners who believe in leading by example and encouraging participation from staff members.

Your team members are a critical asset to the success of your business; they are your family. Treat them with the utmost honor, dignity, and respect. This is not to say that you allow your staff to remain inactive. You can challenge them to become active participants in promoting your company while providing the utmost level of customer service to your clients. They need an effective leader who is going to inspire them and guide them down the road to success.

There were three leadership styles developed by psychologist Kurt Lewin (Lewin, Lippit, and White, 1939).

These styles included the following:

1. Authoritarian (Autocratic) Leadership: These leaders provide clear expectations of what needs to be done. They make decisions independently and demand strict adherence from the followers.
2. Participative (Democratic) Leadership: The leader offers guidance but also asks for input and suggestions from the group before making a decision.
3. Delegative (Laissez-Faire) Leadership: The leaders offer little or no guidance and allow the group to make decisions for themselves.

According to Lewin, the participative style of leadership was the most popular among followers.

Another highly effective form of leadership was proposed by James MacGregor Burns and is called the transformational style of leadership. Under this model, leaders inspire their employees to work toward common goals. As described by Brian Tracy, "Transformational leadership is the ability to motivate, inspire, and bring people to higher levels of performance. Transformational leadership is the ability to touch people emotionally, to empower them to be more and to contribute more than they ever have before."

When you examine effective styles of managing people, it is best to combine both the participative and transformational styles of leadership. This is the way to inspire and motivate your staff to peak performance. When you are able to make them active participants, they will want to excel.

If you are the type of leader who wants to give out orders in a condescending manner, resentment will build and your staff won't have any desire to help you grow and expand your business. On the other hand, if you are supportive and work collaboratively with members of your organization to solve problems, you will build a team of loyal employees who will go above and beyond to ensure your success.

Hiring Process

You need to be very meticulous when hiring in order to find remarkable individuals who will put their entire dedication into the job. During the first, second, and possibly the third interview, people are generally on their best behavior and are not likely to disclose their true identity to you. As a result, the hiring process needs to be more intensive.

During the initial interviewing phase, it might be a good idea to narrow down your search to the top three to five candidates. At this point, invite them to dinner in order to ascertain how they interact in a more casual setting. This type of environment may cause them to lower their protective guard and might give you an idea of their true personality. In addition, this will be a great opportunity to ask them what their long term goals are and where they want to head in life. You can encourage them to bring their spouse, boyfriend, or girlfriend to this meal. By observing their interaction with their partner, you can gain good insight regarding their character.

Think about this for a moment. Isn't it better to invest more time during the hiring process instead of risking the chance of hiring an ineffective employee that you will have to fire in the long run? With a more intensive screening process, you can get a clear indication of whether or not your applicants are going to be committed to the goals and objectives of your company. Closely watch their interaction with other people during this time. Realize that you are hiring an individual that can either hurt you or greatly assist you within your organization.

Steve Harrison takes a very proactive approach to hiring new employees for his company. In addition to interviewing a possible candidate one-on-one, he will give tests to the applicant and will pay them for their time. He focuses on finding someone who will "love the job." He will present them with scenarios and ask the candidate to solve the problems. This might include performing a particular task related to the job for which they are applying. Harrison will give them at least three or four assignments and then compare them to the other applicants. However, if this involves several hours, Steve will pay them for a one day audition. He will only hire passionate people who love their job.

There is another point of consideration when it comes to the hiring process. As an entrepreneur, you need to have an understanding of personality types. Some people are born leaders and will openly embrace any task that is given to them working diligently until they find a solution. Other people are just followers and will remain in the background doing the bare minimum to get by in their jobs. You should strive to find the type of individual who is going to excel, someone who is going to be very active and guided by their own initiative. If you hire an employee that needs to be told every single aspect of doing their job, you will slow down the operation of your business. You want to find a person who works well on their own with little supervision. But don't take their word for it. Before you make the decision to hire them, give some scenarios related to the position they are applying for and ask them how they will effectively resolve the challenges. If they tell you that they will go to their supervisor or manager for direction, then this will give you a good idea of what they will do if you hire them. At this point, remove them as a potential candidate for the job and search for another person.

The Challenge

"As leaders, our job is not to cheerlead our team. Our highest role as a leader is to challenge our people in the higher levels of potential and performance; that challenge itself is the world's greatest motivator, period. Inform them on how to think. It has to be done with real compassion, real care, real service in mind, real heart. They want to know that collectively they're going to accomplish something grand; something meaningful. Your job as a leader is to figure out what that is and then motivating them is as simple as describing that hill and what lies on top."

—Brendon Burchard

For any entrepreneur, business owner, or manager, it becomes a real challenge to hire the best possible person. Understand that a phenomenal team member can greatly improve revenue and profits while an inadequate staff member can be detrimental to your company. For this reason, careful consideration and time must be spent when it comes to hiring great people.

Do not allow yourself to make any judgment on a potential applicant based solely upon one interview. During the first and second interviews, the candidate might present themselves in a manner which doesn't reflect their true identity. There should be a few meetings with a potential candidate. Also, a testing process should be implemented to ascertain the abilities of each applicant.

Anyone who is actively involved in the hiring process can tell you nightmares that followed as the result of hiring the wrong person. Conducting a thorough interview process on a possible candidate can reduce major problems in the future.

When you hire someone who will be a definite asset to your company, you are entering into a mutually beneficial relationship. They can help propel your organization in a very positive direction that will generate substantial revenue and profits. In return, you want to give your valued staff member a great amount of respect and appreciation. When you are able to achieve this relationship, you will have a team that will stay with you for years to come.

Millionaire System for Motivating Employees

*1. Determine what motivates each
of your employees individually.
2. Praise your employees for a great job,
correct their mistakes in a non-critical manner,
and thank them for their contributions to your company.
3. Openly welcome suggestions from team members.*

"There is only one type of motivation and that is self-motivation. If you give me the greatest pep talk, the greatest strategies, the greatest mindset shift, the greatest ways to take action; if I really don't want to do them because I am not motivated, I won't do them. Look for ways to inspire and spark it in people. Find out what motivates each person, what inspires them cause they motivate themselves. One of my employees might be motivated by a check that they get as a bonus, someone else might be motivated by a plaque that they

get, somebody else might be motivated by something bigger than a plaque, someone else might be motivated by a certificate that they get for a donation that was made in their name to their favorite charity. Find out what inspires them, that gets them jazzed up, and then reward them accordingly to what inspires and motivates them; let them tell you."

—James Malinchak

1. Determine what motivates each of your employees individually

As a small business owner, you can ask your employees what motivates them. If you have a big company, you have to take a different approach. As noted by James Malinchak, in a large organization, the department heads should have the responsibility of determining what motivates everyone on their team.

In the past, there was a general assumption that everyone was motivated by money alone. However, it was discovered that money does not motivate everyone.

Russell Brunson tries to determine core motivations that will incentivize his employees. In order to help him accomplish his goals, Russell will give his staff a self-survey and ask them what they are motivated by.

Here are some of the questions that Brunson asks on his survey:

- If you had a hundred dollars, what would you do with that? What would you buy?
- If you had five thousand dollars, what would you do with that?
- If you had ten thousand dollars, what would you do with that?

The answers varied from person to person. It appeared that some people were primarily motivated by actual products instead of getting the cash. Everyone has their own unique motivators that will inspire them to action. As a leader, it is your responsibility to determine what that motivating force is for each person. Brunson went on to say, "Just figure out their driving force, what gets them up in the morning, what gets them excited, and then figure out bonuses based on that specific person that will motivate them."

Don't try to guess what your employee wants; just ask them what they would like to have. By taking this approach to help stimulate your team, you will be showing them that they are valued as members of your organization. As a result, the loyalty and commitment that you receive from them will amaze you.

2. Praise your employees for a great job, correct their mistakes in a non-critical manner, and thank them for their contributions to your company

It is important to let your employees know that you appreciate the hard work they are doing for you. Let's face it. The greatest way to get the best performance from your staff members is to let them know that you are thankful for their contributions to your organization. In addition, it is important to provide your team with praise, support, and encouragement for a job well done.

Whatever energy you project onto your team will come back to you. If you treat them with respect, they will be more likely to go above and beyond their duties. At times, you may have to correct a mistake or inadequate performance level from a staff member. When this happens, ensure that your employee leaves your meeting on a positive note. You don't want them to leave your counseling session feeling like they were criticized. You want them to walk away knowing that they are an asset to your company.

Realize that your staff still needs to be challenged in a diplomatic manner so that they don't allow complacency and lack of interest to become part of their daily routine. If you have an employee who is constantly surfing the internet or sending continuous text messages, they are not acting within your best interest and it might be time for them to seek other employment. Before that point is reached, counsel a troubled member of your organization and attempt to rectify their negative behavior.

If your team member fails to perform as required, there is a systematic approach to resolving the issue. Understand that this should be done in private and not in the presence of other people. When you call an employee in to talk with them regarding an area of concern, here are the steps which should be followed:

1. Give your employee praise for the great job they are doing.
2. Explain their mistake or problematic behavior in a non-critical manner.
3. Provide support and give respect to your employee. Let them know they are a valued member of your business and you appreciate all of their dedication and hard work.

It is imperative that they leave the meeting feeling that you value their contributions to your company. If you are able to accomplish this, they will be more likely to change their problematic behavior. At this point, they will return back to work with a reinvigorated attitude to get things done. When you implement the above steps, you are giving the person a chance to maintain their dignity and they don't feel like they were being attacked. When someone feels like they are being pushed into a corner, the natural tendency is to fight back. However, when the above steps are effectively implemented, the employee walks away realizing they need to correct a mistake or problem but also recognizing that they are respected within your organization. At this point, the loyalty that they develop for you will be strengthened.

The above listed steps can also be used in personal relationships to enhance your interactions with family and friends. At times, we are going to make mistakes and might have a tendency to become complacent. However, we all want to know that we are appreciated by others. If a person feels like they are being attacked emotionally, the first inclination is to fight back and you will not change their behavior. If you approach them from a position of love, the outcome will be very positive.

When you are able to let the other person feel you are treating them with dignity, there is a strong bond created between the two of you. As a result, they will be open and receptive to doing what you want.

3. Openly welcome suggestions from team members

In today's new economy, the old way of doing business doesn't work anymore. Under the old model, a considerable amount of business owners would never consider reaching out to their team members for suggestions or advice. In order to succeed today, this traditional mindset has to be discarded and there needs to be a willingness to accept help and guidance from the staff.

Steve Harrison's company has a very low turnover rate because they are able to create an environment where people enjoy working together. His employees feel that if they do a good job, they're going to get paid more and assume more responsibility. According to Harrison, "We ask for their ideas, advice, and feedback."

Steve sent out an email to his entire staff and gave them an overview of what he was thinking. He told them to picture themselves running the company and asked the following questions:

- What would you get rid of that we're doing now?
- What would you add?
- What would you do differently?
- What do you think that people really want?
- What do you wish we had?

After sending out this email, there was a very positive response with great suggestions. This was followed by a brainstorming meeting with everyone in order to get additional ideas and prioritize what steps should be taken to advance the company forward.

Realize that your employees are involved in the day-to-day operations of your business and are working directly with your customers and clients. As a result, they can provide a unique perspective into what is working and not working. It is easy for an executive or entrepreneur to become so consumed with the operational aspects that they forget about receiving input from their staff but this is the utmost importance.

For the ultimate success of your business, it is imperative that you invite your team to give their suggestions and advice. In addition, be willing to get feedback from your clients and customers. When you ask for help and suggestions, you are building a level of trust and admiration that will strengthen your bond with them. They will walk away feeling that their opinion really matters.

Lessons Learned

"There have to be rewards beyond salary... It is important to have recognition for employees with employee of the month plaques, rewards, time off, vacations, and anything else they need. If they need a day off or a vacation that they are entitled to, let them have it. The more you give to them; they're going to give back to you tenfold... You have to hire people that will find work to do and

they'll go above and beyond what is expected of them... Here is what you want to do to keep your employees motivated: 1. Tell them the good work that they're doing. 2. Reprimand them for the stuff they're doing wrong. 3. Give them something to feel good about so when they leave, they got the clear message but they walk away feeling like they're appreciated in this company."

—Mike Filsaime

Don't lose sight of why you hired your staff; you hired them to help you grow and expand your business. What is the best way to have them help you increase your revenue and profits? You need to get them actively engaged as an integral part of your organization so that they feel their contributions are making a real difference. As a result, they will not view themselves as just an employee; they will view themselves as a treasured member of your family.

Do you actively compliment your team on a job well done? Do you let them know that you are thankful for their help, suggestions, and ideas? If they need time off to attend their child's event at school, do you give it to them without any problem? When you are able to operate from the perspective of your employee and treat them with respect, you will be astonished at the amount of dedication you get from them. They will appreciate you and want to go above and beyond to ensure the victory of your business.

You might want to consider the option of letting your team member work from home one day every week. This small gesture on your part could change the overall attitude and motivation of that person. When you are able to view your associates as unique individuals, then your attitude toward them will change in a positive manner. This is not to say that you permit them to become lazy and not get any work done. They need to be challenged in a diplomatic manner with a non-confrontational tone of voice. Always allow a problem employee to maintain their dignity and give them a chance to correct the problem.

Ask your employees what will motivate them and increase their productivity level. By establishing an open dialogue, you will learn exactly what they want in order for them to perform at their highest level possible.

Mastermind Action Steps:

Action Step #1: Give a survey to your employees and ask what motivates them. You may want to ask them what they would do with a certain amount of money or you may ask them what they would like to have. Find out if they would like to work from home one day a week or if they would like other benefits at the office.

Action Step #2: When you are ready to correct a mistake or problematic behavior for a given employee, talk to them in private. Praise them for the great job they are doing for your business, outline their area of concern in a non-confrontational manner, and thank them for the contributions to your company. Most importantly, let them know that they are a valued member of your family.

Action Step #3: Let your team members know that you actively welcome their suggestions for improving the direction of your business. Send out a survey to your employees and ask them how they would improve your products, services, and customer relations.

"You're never going to motivate anyone until you find out what they want. You have to find out what people want and then you have to work towards helping them get it. That is absolutely essential."
—Bob Proctor

Chapter 10
THE HEART OF A MILLIONAIRE

"Motivation? I love life. Life is a gift. It's the best gift we ever have in our whole world and it's what you make it. If you go through bad times and you feel sorry for yourself, that's your choice, but if you choose to deal with whatever issues you have to, and know that tomorrow the sun is going to come out. It's going to be a beautiful day. Just enjoy every moment that's given to you; you will survive."
—Karolyn Grimes

This chapter will focus on three remarkable individuals who are recognized for their passion and strong desire to push forward even when faced with adversity. The emphasis is not on their financial success; but on their will to succeed when obstacles are thrown into their path. For them, giving up is not an option. They are centered on surviving and overcoming challenges with an unwavering determination. Their passion, willpower, and perseverance are equivalent to all of the respected millionaires presented throughout this book. They have the ability to inspire others and their willingness to give back to other people is highly admirable. Clearly, these three people have the "heart of a millionaire."

At times, life can throw some very challenging barriers into our path. Unfortunately, a number of individuals just give up without making any attempt to overcome the adversities that are encountered. What is the difference between a person who is willing to succeed and someone who just gives up? In this chapter, you will discover the answer to this question. The incredible people featured in the following pages can motivate you through their stories of struggle and accomplishment. Their secrets for reaching optimal success and having a non-stoppable persistence can also be modeled and applied to your own life.

We may not be able to control the obstacles that are thrown into our path but we can decide how we respond to these difficulties. Our strong will to move onward with a positive focus on the future will help to ensure our victory. Ultimately, the manner in which we perceive setbacks and the decision to stop or continue forward will determine our eventual success or failure. The individuals spotlighted in this chapter demonstrate that it is possible to endure any hardship which may arise on our journey through life.

This chapter will highlight the following respected individuals:

- Captain "Sully" Sullenberger who was responsible for landing US Airways Flight 1549 on the Hudson River after both engines were lost just after takeoff.
- Actress Karolyn Grimes who starred with Jimmy Stewart and Donna Reed in the movie, *"It's a Wonderful Life."*
- Julie Clark, a retired Northwest Airlines Captain, was one of the very first female captains for a major commercial airline and she is also a highly accomplished aerobatic pilot.

It should be noted that scheduling conflicts would not permit an interview with Captain Sully but special permission was granted to include him in this chapter.

Captain Chesley "Sully" Sullenberger... A True Hero

"Mayday, mayday, mayday... Hit birds. We've lost thrust in both engines. We're turning back towards LaGuardia... I did not think I was going to die. Based on my experience, I was confident that I could make an emergency water landing that was survivable. That confidence was stronger than any fear... It was vital that I be focused, and that I allow myself no distractions. My consciousness existed solely to control the flight path."

—**Captain Chesley "Sully" Sullenberger**,
Highest Duty: My Search for What Really Matters

Captain Chesley "Sully" Sullenberger gained public notoriety in 2009 when there was a major incident that made worldwide news and elevated Sully from captain to hero within a matter of minutes. After this happened, we were given the opportunity of getting to know Captain Sullenberger through his media appearances, books that he wrote, and his willingness to join his co-pilot, Jeff Skiles, as Co-Chairmen of the Young Eagles Program which introduces children to the world of aviation. The public discovered that Sully is a highly committed individual who put the safety of his passengers and crew above his own safety. His vigilance during a crisis situation was the key element that allowed him to save 155 people on board the plane in addition to the countless people who were on the ground. As you continue reading, be inspired by Sully's perseverance and commitment to reaching a successful outcome.

On January 15th, 2009, US Airways Captain Chesley "Sully" Sullenberger received clearance from air traffic control to takeoff from LaGuardia Airport in New York; the flight was bound for Charlotte, North Carolina. Captain Sully, a former United States Air Force fighter pilot, was sitting in the pilot's seat of US Airways Flight 1549 alongside First Officer Jeff Skiles. The plane that they were flying was an Airbus A320 and there were 155 passengers and crew on board.

It began as a perfectly normal flight but Captain Sully and his crew encountered a major crisis that could not be anticipated. This is a day that will forever go down in aviation history as the greatest miraculous achievement by a commercial airline pilot. The media referred to Sullenberger as a hero for his courageous actions. However, Sully did not view himself as a hero. In his mind, he was simply taking responsibility as a captain for the safety of his passengers and crew members.

As the US Airways plane took off and started to climb, a major problem erupted: only ninety seconds into the flight, the plane struck a flock of Canadian Geese. Can you picture the geese hitting the plane and the birds going into the engines? At this point, both engines were lost. For any pilot, losing thrust in both engines at a low altitude and speed over a densely populated area becomes a major concern. From an aerodynamic perspective, the airplane lost forward momentum, stopped climbing, and began to slow down. Almost instantly, Sully had to gain control over the aircraft as it began to make the descent back to the ground.

"Within eight seconds of the bird strike, realizing that we were without engines, I knew that this was the worst aviation challenge I'd ever faced. It was the most sickening, pit-of-your-stomach, falling-through-the-floor feeling I had ever experienced. I knew immediately and intuitively that I needed to be at the controls," wrote Captain Sully in his book, *Highest Duty: My Search for What Really Matters*.

Decisions had to be made very quickly regarding this sudden and unexpected emergency. Upon initial communication with air traffic control, Captain Sully states that he hit birds, lost thrust in both engines, and he will be returning back to LaGuardia. All departures out of LaGuardia were stopped by air traffic control. At that moment, Sullenberger was thinking quickly and examined all available options. He realized that a return to LaGuardia was impossible. He calmly told the air traffic controller that he was unable to land on the runway and they may end up in the Hudson.

Sullenberger asked about landing at Teterboro Airport in New Jersey. The controller received permission to clear US Airways to land on runway one. At this point, Sullenberger can be heard saying, "We can't do it." Shortly after that, you hear the following, "We're going to be in the Hudson."

Sully knew that he couldn't fly the plane back to LaGuardia and he also realized that he couldn't make it to Teterboro. His only viable option was to land the plane on the Hudson River but this presented an entirely new set of challenges. In order to make a successful water landing, Sully had to keep the wings exactly level with the nose of the plane slightly up. In addition, he needed to touchdown just above his minimum flying speed but not below it and maintain a descent rate that would be as safe as possible.

Can you begin to imagine the amount of fear that anyone would have if they were unexpectedly thrown into this situation? Throughout the entire transmission between Captain Sully and the air traffic controller, there were no visible signs of fear or distress in the voice of Captain Sullenberger. His professionalism and many years of flight experience were clearly evident.

Captain Sullenberger had no other alternative but to carefully land the US Airways plane on the Hudson River and this incident become known as "Miracle on the Hudson." Some people might say that he was a trained pilot and prepared for emergency situations like that. Yes, his countless hours of logged flight time would make him a more experienced pilot but no one had imagined that a pilot would have to land a major commercial airline on the Hudson River.

Commercial airline pilots will utilize flight simulators in order to increase their proficiency and help them prepare for possible emergencies. However, in flight simulator exercises, it was not possible to practice a water landing because the simulators weren't programmed for that type of emergency scenario. Thus, the only training available came from a theoretical classroom discussion.

How in the world can anyone prepare for losing both engines just after takeoff and having to land a commercial airliner in the Hudson River? When faced with a crisis situation, the most important tasks must be prioritized with all effort, energy, and attention being directed toward the greatest area of concern.

As humans, we are all subject to normal emotional responses during high pressure situations. There are many experienced pilots who faced with the exact same circumstances would have crashed their plane. What is the unique element that sets Captain Sullenberger apart from other people who are thrown into a crisis situation? Simply stated, Sully pushed his fear to the side, focused on taking decisive action, and was confident that he would be successful. For Sullenberger, there was only one option; to safely land the plane on the river.

Sully's extensive flight experience, training, and background would have been useless if he allowed himself to become paralyzed by fear. If we allow fear to consume us, then we cannot do what needs to be done and this can have a devastating outcome. When both engines were lost, Sully immediately pushed any fear to the side and focused his attention on safely landing the plane. Seconds were of the essence and all his concentration was on making a safe water landing. Not only were the lives of everyone on board Flight 1549 in jeopardy, but the safety of the people on the ground was another issue of concern.

Captain Sullenberger landed the plane on the Hudson River and everyone was evacuated. After this, even as water was filling the interior of the cabin, Sully walked down the aisle of the entire US Airways Airbus twice to ensure that all passengers and crew members were safely off the plane. At this point, the safety of everyone else was a top priority.

Sully's experience is spotlighted to show that you can overcome any major obstacle that is encountered in life. As long as you are able to push fear to the side and proceed forward with a determined attitude knowing you will be successful, nothing will stop you from reaching what you want to accomplish.

Sullenberger also gives recognition to his crew members who were on board Flight 1549. He credits First Officer Jeff Skiles and his flight crew for working effectively as a team. As a result, they were essential for helping Sully achieve a successful outcome.

Clearly, Captain Sully's actions were heroic and highly commendable. His willingness to push through an emergency situation while putting the safety of his passengers and crew above himself distinguishes Sully as a remarkable individual who holds the "heart of a millionaire" deep within his soul.

Lessons Learned

In order to attain success, you need to:

1. Push through any challenging situation in a calm manner.
2. Develop a plan and consider all available options.
3. Maintain vigilance and be prepared for the unexpected.
4. Discard fear.

5. Avoid complacency and take decisive action.
6. Have total belief and confidence in yourself and your decisions.
7. Be focused on reaching a positive outcome.

Captain Sully is involved with several worthwhile charities. Two of them will be discussed in this chapter:

1. EAA Young Eagles Program
2. St. Jude Children's Research Hospital

Co-Chairman of EAA Young Eagles
Captain Sully is admired and respected within the aviation community. Sullenberger and Jeff Skiles were Co-Chairmen of the Experimental Aircraft Association (EAA) Young Eagles program, launched in 1992 in Oshkosh, Wisconsin. The purpose of the program is to introduce children, between the ages of 8 to 17, to the opportunity of experiencing flight in general aviation. Flights are offered free of charge and are provided by EAA volunteers. Under this program, there have been more than 1.9 million Young Eagle flights.

Sully's concern for helping children explore a passion for aviation is admirable and makes him a great leader. Captain Sullenberger and Jeff Skiles stepped down as co-chairmen of EAA Young Eagles in 2013 when Sean D. Tucker became the Young Eagles Chairman.

http://www.youngeagles.org/

St. Jude Children's Research Hospital
Captain Sully is also actively involved with St. Jude Children's Research Hospital, founded in 1962 by actor and entertainer, Danny Thomas. It was named after Saint Jude Thaddeus. Danny Thomas believed in the power of prayer and promised St. Jude that if he became successful, he would build a shrine to honor St. Jude. Well, he kept his promise and

St. Jude Children's Research Hospital was built. The hospital provides medical treatment to children who are dealing with catastrophic diseases regardless of a family's ability to pay.

http://www.stjude.org

For more information on Captain Chesley "Sully" Sullenberger, visit his website at: http://sullysullenberger.com/

Karolyn Grimes – A Wonderful Life

"I knew that my life was just beginning and that it would get better.
I would visualize what would make me happy.
I really knew that this was temporary and I would get through it."

—**Karolyn Grimes**

You may not be familiar with Karolyn Grimes or you may know her as ZuZu Bailey from the movie, *"It's A Wonderful Life,"* which starred Jimmy Stewart. If you watched the movie, you will remember her as the adorable little girl who became well known for her catch phrase, "Look daddy, teacher says, every time a bell rings, an angel gets his wings."

When you consider the best Christmas movies of all time, the 1946 major motion picture by Frank Capra, *"It's A Wonderful Life,"* will definitely be at the top of the list. This movie starred James Stewart, Donna Reed, Henry Travers, and Karolyn Grimes. The movie is focused on a man, George Bailey (James Stewart), who doesn't realize the dramatic impact that he had in the lives of his family and friends. His guardian angel, Clarence Odbody (Henry Travers), showed George all the lives that he affected in a positive manner and how different things would have been if he had never been born.

Grimes had the great honor of working directly with Jimmy Stewart. "I truly think he was a very kind and gentle man. I think he truly tried to build a little chemistry between us and it was very nice. He was always patient and I really liked him a lot. I'm the perennial daughter in the movie life for him," Karolyn recalled. Forty years after the movie was produced, Karolyn was able to reconnect with Jimmy Stewart and they became close until Stewart passed away on July 2, 1997.

She had many great memories working on the movie. "I really did like the Christmas tree and I enjoyed playing with the other kids. Plus, I really enjoyed the snow because it may not have been real but I was born and raised in Hollywood. It doesn't snow there," stated Karolyn. She continued, "We were disciplined. When the red light went on, that was the sign you were still. You don't make a noise or you don't last too long in that business because they lose money."

The movie had a very happy ending but for Karolyn Grimes, in her real life, she did not have a picture perfect life as portrayed on the major motion picture screen. To the contrary, she faced many adversities.

As a child, Karolyn had a very promising acting career and worked with the top names in Hollywood including John Wayne, Cary Grant, Bing Crosby, Fred MacMurray, Danny Kaye, and Loretta Young. However, her acting career came to an abrupt end when both of her parents died. Her mother died from Alzheimer's disease and her father was killed in a traffic accident. After this, she had to move to Missouri in order to live with her aunt and uncle.

Sadly, the life with her aunt and uncle was not a happy one. Her aunt appeared to be a righteous and decent person but this wasn't the truth. She was an uncaring, mean, and nasty person who tormented Karolyn with constant psychological abuse. On the other hand, her uncle was very quiet and withdrawn in regards to the mental abuse that his wife projected onto his niece. This was just the beginning of a life filled with many hardships for Karolyn.

One of the biggest saving graces was the encouraging support that Karolyn received from her neighbors and business owners in the town where she lived. They gave her love, strength, and showed Karolyn genuine care.

Subsequently, Grimes went to college but had to leave without graduating because of continued psychological trauma from her aunt. "My aunt started stalking me at college; a little hard for me to stomach so I ended up quitting before I actually got my degree. I got married so that I could just get away from her and that was the wrong thing to do but it got me out of her clutches all the way," said Karolyn. The marriage ended in divorce but she had two children with her husband. Certainly, this was another very difficult period in her life but in spite of the stresses, she became a medical technician.

Karolyn then married her second husband and she was a mom to a total of seven children which included the following: a step mom to her husband's three children, two of her own children, and she had another two children with her new husband. In addition to being a mother, she also worked as a medical technician.

During this time, one of the worst possible tragedies hit her and the family. Her son committed suicide at the age of eighteen. How in the world could Karolyn overcome the death of her child? "I had an inner strength once again. I just knew that I had to get through it and I had other kids that I had to be strong for and I had to prevent that from happening to them." Karolyn continued, "I couldn't dwell on my pain. I had to just get through it. It was really hard at first but I healed." Three years after her son's suicide, her husband died of lung cancer.

Karolyn's setbacks continued when a financial adviser gave her bad advice and she lost a lot of money in the stock market. "I called the broker when it had dropped below a million dollars. Don't you think you should get me out of the market? He talked me out of it. When it dropped to $800,000, don't you think you should get me out of the market? He talked me out of it again," said Karolyn. In the end, she lost a total of $700,000 and the collapse of the real estate market plunged her into major financial distress.

Her negative experience with her broker is a lesson for everyone. Karolyn knew intuitively that her money should be removed from the market but she deferred to the expertise of the broker. She lost a significant amount of money because she trusted the wrong person. Learn from this and take responsibility for your financial destiny by doing your homework and careful planning in regards to your own investing. When you become creative and diversify or spread your money across several types of investments, you will minimize any potential loss. Simply put, you work hard to get your money; you should also spend time investing it wisely.

In Hollywood today, the actors and actresses are entitled to receive residual compensation for their acting jobs. However, this was not the case in 1946. The actors received a one-time payment for their role. Even though *"It's a Wonderful Life"* continued to grow in popularity over the years, Karolyn does not receive any type of residuals for her work on the movie.

How could Grimes endure all of the adversities that were thrown into her path? She knew that these traumatic events were only temporary and she would make it through them. She stressed the importance of "having faith, family, and friends." Karolyn said, "We are so fortunate to have life and I appreciate that. I have a lot of gratitude that I can get up every morning. I'm here for another day."

Grimes faced many challenges throughout her lifetime but she proceeded forward and overcame the difficulties in her path. Through it all, Karolyn maintains a healthy and upbeat attitude. She is a happy and content person who shares her love with other people, and she is the "unofficial ambassador" for the movie, *"It's a Wonderful Life."*

Karolyn enjoys making public appearances and promoting the movie. This gives her the opportunity of sharing behind the scene stories from the movie set. The movie conveys a message of love and concern for other people. Without a doubt, the main character, George Bailey, cared about his neighbors and friends. Similarly, Karolyn cares about other people and she loves sharing the positive message of the movie with fans.

As we hear a bell ring, angels get their wings and our challenge is to push forward with optimism. In the movie, Clarence Odbody AS2 (Angel Second Class) showed George Bailey and all of us that we impact other people's lives in positive ways that we could never imagine. Throughout our life, the contact that we have with other people can play a dramatic importance even though it might not be realized. For this reason, treat others with the utmost dignity, respect, and love. Leave everyone you come into contact with a memorable impression of you regardless of how limited your time is with them.

Karolyn's story needed to be shared in this chapter. For anyone who believes that they can't withstand misfortunes in life, just take a look at what Karolyn encountered. In spite of all her negative experiences, she always maintained a positive outlook. Be willing to embrace the same refreshing attitude that Karolyn displayed when any challenging event is thrown into your path. Clearly, Karolyn Grimes has the heart and soul of a millionaire.

Lessons Learned

In order to ensure a happy outcome and have a wonderful life, you need to:

1. Make the commitment and decision to take action, proceed forward, and never lose sight of what is important to you.

2. Don't become obsessed over hardships; your setbacks in life are only temporary and will pass in time.
3. When you face obstacles, look ahead and focus on a positive outcome.
4. Keep centered on what you want to accomplish.

To learn more about Karolyn, please visit: http://www.zuzu.net/

Captain Julie Clark – Nothing Stood in Her Way

"You meet people who have no idea what it means to set goals requiring so much time, effort, and expense. They don't know what hard work is all about. On the other hand, they miss the thrill of achievement and the pleasure of coming into contact with the great people who help you along the way."

—Captain Julie Clark
Nothing Stood In Her Way

Julie Clark is a highly admired aerobatic pilot and retired airline captain from Northwest Airlines. She encountered many challenges throughout her life but she maintained a steadfast determination to be successful. During her childhood, her mom passed away and her dad was shot to death. Julie then decided to pursue a career in aviation when the only women in the field were stewardesses. Captain Clark entered into a profession that was dominated by men at a time when the airlines were not anxious to hire their first female pilot.

Julie had additional challenges within her personal life. She fell in love with the man of her dreams but their marriage ended in divorce when she discovered her husband was cheating. After that, she fell in love again with another man, Tony, who died in an airplane accident.

Then, she married an individual who stole money from her and this marriage also ended in divorce.

She also encountered setbacks within her business. Her treasurer stole a substantial amount of money from her business and she almost lost her aerobatic company when the FAA (Federal Aviation Administration) grounded her type of airplane which was used for aerobatics. Through it all, she maintained a positive outlook and "nothing stood in her way" of accomplishing her dream.

"God Bless the USA" is the Lee Greenwood song playing over the public address system across the airfield as Julie Clark performs her aerobatic routine in her Beechcraft T-34 Mentor, nicknamed "Wally." As you look to the sky, you will find the red, white, and blue smoke trailing behind her T-34. Her aerobatic performance has amazed countless spectators who enjoy the beauty of her seamless routine which is executed precisely.

Spectators who watch her performance appreciate Julie's great talent as an aerobatic pilot. However, Julie had many obstacles to overcome before she reached this point. When she was only fourteen, her mother passed away. "I heard them telling me that my mother had choked to death. Mom was gone. Gone! I wanted them to be wrong. I wanted to scream. I wanted them to be wrong, terribly, dreadfully wrong!" she wrote in her book, *Nothing Stood in Her Way.*

At the age of fifteen, Julie would endure another tragedy in her life, the murder of her dad. Her father, Ernie Clark, was an airline captain. He was flying Pacific Airlines flight 773 with a co-pilot, flight attendant, and forty passengers on board. During the flight, a gunman pushed his way into the cockpit and shot Ernie Clark to death. After this, even though it is believed that the co-pilot struggled with the gunman, the plane still crashed and everyone on board was killed. Ironically, her father was not scheduled to fly that day; he was covering a shift for someone who called off sick.

"After my dad's airplane crash, I remember thinking, I'll never get to fly in an airplane again because I loved flying with him and I just loved airplanes. I always knew I would want to learn to fly and I just figured my dad would teach me. So, the desire, the bug, and the seed was already planted before he died," stated Julie.

After experiencing these hardships, Julie still held the dream of becoming a commercial airline pilot deep within her heart and soul. She maintained persistence and kept moving forward. Julie became an air hostess (flight attendant) for TWA (Trans World Airlines) and then with World Airways. When she was flying overseas and the movie was playing for the passengers, Julie was in the cockpit talking to the pilots.

Sacrifice and commitment were required on the part of Captain Clark before her dream could become a reality. Her day started at 6am and ended at 2am. She would begin by taking flying lessons in the morning at San Carlos Airport in California. After that, she would go to her job at Marine World which was water skiing and then head over to Charley Brown Steakhouse in the evening to work as a waitress.

In the 1960's, it was somewhat unusual for a woman to pursue a career as a commercial airline pilot but this did not stop Julie. She had a dream that she wanted to achieve and Julie worked hard in order to ensure that she reached her dream of becoming a pilot.

It is costly to take flying lessons and achieve the ratings required to become a commercial airline pilot. Now it was time for Captain Clark to become creative in order to finance her flying lessons. She came up with the innovative idea of starting her very own clock business, Jule's Clocks. She would buy clocks for $15 in lots of fifty, restore them, and do any necessary repairs. After this, she was able to sell each clock for anywhere from $100 to $150. Julie could easily make an average of $1,000 in one day just by selling ten clocks. This small business allowed her to pay for her flight training and it triggered her entrepreneurial spirit.

Jule's Clocks was just the beginning for Captain Clark. In 1980, she formed her business, American Aerobatics, and incorporated it in 1989. She had sponsorship and moved in a positive direction with incorporation but she made a mistake when she appointed a very close and trusted person as treasurer of the company. He was given access to all of the money and authority to sign checks for the business. When a $70,000 check came in from a sponsor, the treasurer endorsed it, deposited it into the business account, and then wrote a check to himself for that amount. At that moment, the money was gone forever. This was a wake-up call for Julie. She learned an important lesson from that bad experience but she kept moving onward.

Captain Clark was able to get smaller jobs flying as a pilot but her big break came when she was finally able to get a position with Golden West Airlines. "That truly was the hardest job I've ever had to try to get. Nobody wanted to hire their first woman pilot," said Clark. She passed her check ride with the chief pilot, Captain August, and completed the physical, but they still wouldn't hire her yet. The men's bathroom didn't have a door and the chief pilot had a concern regarding this issue. The bathroom was located in the ramp office of LAX (Los Angeles Airport) and this was the location for pilots to meet their crew, get weather briefings, prepare for their flights, and use the bathroom if needed. Prior to 1976, women were never an issue regarding this matter. At this point, in a firm manner, Julie told Captain August that she would buy the door and install it on the bathroom if he gave her the job. August respected her determined attitude and she was hired as their first and only woman pilot for Golden West Airlines.

Julie broke through a major barrier and opened the door for other women to become pilots. At this time, she received very positive feedback from her colleagues. According to Captain Clark, "I made kinship with a lot of captains. I got letters from World Airways pilots and TWA pilots that were so thrilled to know that I was now an airline pilot." She was one of the very first female airline pilots for a commercial airline. Later on, she became a captain for Northwest Airlines.

The very first female hired by a commercial airline was Emily Warner who worked for Frontier Airlines and subsequently earned her captain's wings. Warner also became the first president of the International Social Affiliation of Women Airline Pilots, also known as ISA plus 21. It was an organization formed by the first twenty-one women pilots of which Captain Clark was a charter member.

As Julie was starting to grow a successful aerobatic business, there was a crash at an air combat school and all T-34's were grounded by the FAA (Federal Aviation Administration). This meant that Julie could not perform aerobatic routines in her T-34 and she came very close to losing a major sponsor and her business. At this point, Captain Clark had to fight to keep her entrepreneurial dream alive. She made a personal trip to Washington D.C. to meet with Jane Garvey who was head of the FAA. In a firm and diplomatic manner, Julie explained her case to Garvey. She felt that she was unfairly being placed into the same category as the air combat schools just because she flew the same type of airplane. This was not a true reflection upon Julie or the T-34 that she was flying during her performances. She was always concerned about safety and ensured that her plane was subjected to meticulous care and regular maintenance. Subsequently, Clark was able to get a waiver to fly her Beechcraft T-34. If she wouldn't have fought to keep her plane flying, she might have lost everything.

Although Captain Clark faced many hardships and obstacles, she never gave up on her ultimate objective; becoming a commercial airline pilot. Her commitment, dedication, and persistence clearly indicate a person who holds a dream deep within their heart and soul. Some people, when presented with setbacks, just turn and walk away. For

Julie, this was never an option. She would not let anything stand in the way of reaching her goals.

Over the years, you may have become sidetracked and given up on your hopes and dreams. For whatever reason, your passion for achieving your dreams may have disappeared. But there is hope!

You can rekindle the passion for the goal you once held. It is possible to get that feeling back but you must make the decision now. You must decide that you want to achieve your goals without having any hesitancy or uncertainty. Consider this. If you permit yourself the opportunity of getting excited all over again for that dream that you once held deep within your heart and soul, your high level of enthusiasm and excitement will start to return. As a result, a vibrational energy will begin to radiate throughout your mind and body thereby launching you toward reaching all of your aspirations.

At times you may get knocked down in life but you need to keep getting up and progressing forward. Julie Clark is a wonderful example of someone who was able to do this. For anything of significance in life, you have to be willing to work for it. Throughout it all, Julie never gave up on her dreams.

Currently, Julie is retired from Northwest Airlines but she is very active with her aerobatic business. She performs at numerous airshows every year but you can always find her in Oshkosh, Wisconsin every summer for the annual EAA (Experimental Aircraft Association) airshow called AirVenture.

Julie also has a strong passion and concern for the safety of animals. She supports the SPCA (Society for the Prevention of Cruelty to Animals) and her real love is for the protection of marine life animals.

Nothing Stood in Her Way is the name of her book and the philosophy that Captain Clark has towards life. Clearly, her willingness and dedication to push through all adversities is the same rock solid spirit held by all the millionaires within the pages of this book. Julie might not be a millionaire but she holds the true heart and soul of a millionaire deep inside. She is a great role model and inspiration for anyone who wants to pursue their dreams in life.

Lessons Learned

Here are the steps that Julie utilized to become successful:

1. Realize that setbacks are a normal part of life.
2. Be willing to stand up for your dream and push through all obstacles.
3. Be ready to defend your dream in a firm and diplomatic manner without giving up.
4. Have a firm commitment to reaching your goals.

For more information on Julie Clark, please visit:
http://www.julieclarkairshows.com

Chapter 11

BREAKTHROUGH TO FINANCIAL AND EMOTIONAL WEALTH

"When you wake up, you get up. You make a commitment, you keep it, and you study every day. I don't hit a snooze button. I get up and I get going."

—Bob Proctor

I n this chapter, we'll look at a major breakthrough that each millionaire experienced. These breakthroughs helped to skyrocket them to a higher intellectual level, greater emotional awareness, and were instrumental for their overall success.

At different points throughout our lifetime, we all have moments that could be called breakthroughs. However, it is how we perceive these events and if we decide to take action that will determine our eventual outcome and victory.

Success = Helping Others

When you are able to develop your skills in a way that can help other people, you can guarantee a career that will last for many years. You have a talent and gift to share with others. Don't pursue a job based upon the huge amount of money you expect to make. Think about your inner passion and dreams. If you get creative, you will find a way that you can make a great living from it. There are a lot of people that absolutely hate their jobs. They are just working for that paycheck every two weeks. But money alone cannot bring you true happiness and inner peace. There are some very wealthy people who are depressed and feel like they have no purpose in life. However, when you are able to help others, the inner satisfaction will be tremendous.

Here are the defining breakthrough moments for each of the highlighted millionaires in this book.

Bob Proctor

Author, Speaker, Consultant, Coach, and Mentor

Bob Proctor was not born into wealth; he was a high school dropout and did not have any money. Bob had to find a creative way to survive. He discovered a book by Napolean Hill called *Think and Grow Rich* which had a transformative influence on his life.

Proctor started cleaning offices and his awakening came when he passed out in the street one day. He thought the answer to making more money was to clean more offices. "I was working so hard, I was exhausted, and I was only about 27 or 28 years old. I couldn't do anymore work. I thought the answer was work harder," Bob recalled. "I think my breakthrough came when I realized that working wasn't going to do it. Hard work wasn't going to do it. I had to leverage myself. I had to share it with other people. I think that was probably the biggest thing I ever learned. I read it but I didn't really understand it until that day I passed out," said Bob.

Proctor referenced a quote from Napolean Hill, "If you believe that hard work and honesty alone will bring riches, perish the thought! It is not true! Riches come, if they come at all, in response to definite demands, based upon the application of definite principles, and not by chance or luck."

Bob quit cleaning offices and he got other people to do what he was doing because "there was a need." As stated by Bob, "I was teaching people how to earn money cleaning offices. I never talked to them about cleaning offices. I talked to them about goals; getting new cars, new houses. I'd just go from one building to the next and keep talking to the cleaners. I was motivating the cleaners." However, this was just the beginning for Proctor because he made the decision to walk away from the business.

"I was going to work with Earl Nightingale and I was in awe of this man. When I got working with him, I found that he was the same as you or me or anybody else. That's when I kept studying. I kept changing my belief about what I could do. I would get this idea, step out, do it, and it worked. And then, I'd do another thing and it worked," said Proctor.

Bob referenced three important qualities for being successful:

1. Integrity - You have to have integrity. You've got to do what you say and say what you do. Your thoughts, your feelings, and actions are all in sync.
2. Give - You have to be very generous with your money, with your time, and with your knowledge. If we give, we receive. You have to willingly give.
3. Receive - You have to graciously receive too.

Brendon Burchard
Author, Motivational Speaker, and High Performance Trainer

Several years ago, Brendon had a car accident and this was his major breakthrough for the overall direction of his life. This was his defining moment and he openly embraced the lesson to be learned from this shocking experience.

In his business, there was a separate breakthrough of great importance which permitted him to discover three critical areas:

1. Distinction – Focusing on: How can I add a different sort of value to the marketplace? How can I be different than the rest of the world? How can the value that we bring to people be distinct and different?
2. Excellence – How can you bring more excellence to everything that we do? How can we heighten the level of operational excellence we have within our business? How can we make sure that our customers in the marketplace see our brand as an excellence driven brand, that they know that whatever they're going to experience with us is going to be top of the charts, top of the line?
3. Service – There's two components of service:
   a. How we serve other people from the heart; living from the heart and operating our business with compassion, empathy, and care for our clients.
   b. The other side of service is customer service; hitting high degrees of excellence and distinction in our customer service.

Brendon's enthusiasm and high energy level is self-evident when you talk to him. "I believe in high performance. High performance versus peak performance is this: it's heightened and sustained. We need to reach a higher level of performance and that means sustained energy," said Brendon. Also, he is centered on "aliveness." As stated by Brendon, "To have within us a sense of heightened energy, engagement, and enthusiasm. What I often call the charge; that's just a sense of aliveness, a sense of aliveness in the moment, a sense of aliveness with other people. When you're around someone who is alive, they're energized, they're engaged, they're enthusiastic or fully charged, that person you want to be around."

Brendon is also very concerned about his customers and clients. "Compassion and love for the people in my life, to the people that I get to serve every day. The most successful people in the world have a deep core to them of empathy that they really care about other people's experiences, feelings, and emotions," Brendon said.

Burchard is focused with his life. As noted by Brendon, "My aim with my life is I don't spend any time doing things that I don't believe will be of service in my professional career. If I just don't think it's going to be something that's real, or something that's going to serve other people, I just bow out of it because time is so short." He continued, "Time is of the essence for us to really live our lives and contribute our gifts."

Mark Victor Hansen
Co-Author of Chicken Soup for the Soul, Keynote Speaker, and Marketing Expert

Mark described his breakthrough moment, "My flash is when I went bankrupt; that was a great benefit. I didn't see it at the time exactly what I should have been doing 40 years ago." Several years ago, he was living in Hicksville Long Island, New York with four roommates. Mark's desire was to speak and he wanted to figure out if there were any speakers who were not lawyers, doctors, or celebrities. His roommate, John, said that there was a guy speaking in Long Island, New York. Mark went to this seminar and was there for three hours. Mark wanted to know how he did it. The speaker shared valuable information with Mark that greatly helped him.

"By breaking down, I could break through. Breakdowns or breakthroughs if you understand that failure always needs work clothes on if you get out of the hole. If you're going to get out of a hole, you've got to dig some steps and get yourself out of the hole," said Mark.

Hansen has a very definite focus:

1. Make sure your vibration is consistent, meaning that we're in a vibratory world rather than a physical world. You're crystal clear what you want.
2. The universe only says yes.
3. If you vibrate at the level of what you want, you get it.

Mark summarized his theory for being successful on this life journey, "Success is being fully who you are. Success is doing what you really want in your heart of hearts with whom you want that you resonate with totally and absolutely, and then achieving full fulfillment of everything that you want."

He is very clear on his purpose and mission. Mark said that you give ten, save ten, invest ten, and then live on the remaining seventy percent of your income. His book series, *Chicken Soup for the Soul*, has done tremendous. "One of the reasons *Chicken Soup* is more successful than any other book is that we pre-decide who we're going to tithe to and then have done it. Then, we do cause related charity work," said Mark. He is committed to helping other people and believes in tithing. His willingness to share with other people is highly admirable.

Mark Victor Hansen continues to maintain a positive vibrational energy even though he has attained substantial success. "I've sold a half a billion books. My goal is to sell a billion, so I'm only halfway to go. Most people say, you're so successful, why don't you quit? Well, why I would want to quit? I'm having a ball," stated Mark.

Sean D. Tucker
Aerobatic Pilot and Chairman of EAA Young Eagles Program

Sean is known as a highly respected aerobatic pilot. However, in 1979, Sean was forced to bail out of his airplane before it crashed. "The accident in '79 was a wake-up call but the taking ownership of all my actions through my entire life was the epiphany that changed my career. And this happened probably in about '84 when I took total ownership for every mistake I've made, for every blunder in my life, total ownership and total responsibility, total accountability was an epiphany and I was set free, absolutely free. I could accomplish anything," said Tucker.

This major awakening for Sean was the catalyst that propelled him forward to the high level of success that he experienced throughout his aerobatic career. As noted by Sean, "The accident was a wake-up call. It made me grow up... I had to build my dream back up, buy new airplanes. I had to start a whole complete different business. Having that wake-up call, and then taking ownership of why I made those mistakes was the epiphany that changed my life."

With a strong passion in his voice, Sean continued, "By '86, I was committed, convicted, and I mean rocking on all cylinders and I was no longer worrying about judgment from other people because I was so successful in my soul and strong in my belief in myself that I felt I could accomplish anything."

Sean also recognizes the importance of other key factors which elevated him to a higher emotional and intellectual level:

1. Employees will give you their heart and soul if you can guarantee them security. They want to know their check is going to clear on the first and fifteenth.
2. The more wealth you share with the people that help you get there; the more wealth you're going to receive in return.
3. Our job on earth is to make the world a better place and through our example, through our good works, and through our sharing of all our knowledge and abilities.
4. The power of the human spirit is you can achieve anything you really in your gut know you're supposed to have, that is your destiny. You always achieve your destiny, so it's up to you to define your destiny.
5. Every success I have, I would visualize.

James Malinchak

Business and Motivational Speaker, Marketing Coach, and Speaker Coach

James had a major breakthrough which propelled his business forward. He said, "My business started to have a breakthrough when I started thinking like a marketing person rather than a doer of the thing. I always say, you're not in the plumbing business; you are in the business of marketing your plumbing services. You're not a speaker; you are in the business of marketing your speaker services. You're not an author; you're in the business of marketing that book. You're not a house painter; you're not a (fill in the blank), you're in the business of marketing that stuff." James continued, "So, you've got to 'Always Be Marketing' (ABM)."

He had a message to share with other people but discovered a major element when he realized that he was "in the business" of marketing his speaker services. It was this mind shift which allowed James to skyrocket his business. He is a speaker, trainer, and coach. However, without any clients, Malinchak wouldn't have a career. So, the importance of always marketing himself in the areas of his expertise elevated his business to a much higher level.

When James started to research speakers and found statistics showing that most of them weren't financially secure, he decided to take responsibility for his own destiny. "I went and started studying marketing, took it, and applied it to speaking. So, the marketing was a major breakthrough for me," said James. "I always said, don't think like a blank; think like a marketer," stated James.

In Chapter 6, the following aspects were briefly mentioned but will be described in further detail here. There are three important elements which Malinchak referenced for being successful:

1. Mindset – It's not positive wishful thinking; it's not pie in the sky wishful thinking. It's not sitting on the couch in a lotus position going um, um, um; I hope the windows open up and customers, prospects, more income, more success, more joy, more fulfillment whatever that might be; I hope it comes to me by this wishful thinking... Changing your mindset. That means thinking differently on a daily, weekly, monthly, and yearly basis; training yourself to think differently.

2. Skillset – You have to do something... Developing a skill set and actually working at that skill set to get better and better and putting sweat equity in when it's not easy. When you don't want to do it, when it doesn't feel good, when you'd rather go do something else. Well, that's what you really have to do to be successful, but nobody wants to do it because it's work and nobody likes to work even though we know we have to.

3. Get off Your Assets – You've got to get off your assets and do something about it. You have to actually take action on it.

Russell Brunson
Internet Marketing Training

"I've been online. I was trying to figure this whole thing out and I don't know what I was doing for eighteen months. I was trying to make money and just never did, and then somewhere along the line I had this idea where I just needed my own product, so I created my own product and boom, instantly, I started making money. That was my big first aha," stated Russell. This was just the beginning for his breakthrough.

Russell openly admits that he had other breakthroughs which included his discovery of the following three elements:

1. Selling product after product, the importance of having product funnels where you have an upsell and downsell.
2. Utilizing automated webinars in order to make the same amount of money with less stress, effort, and people.
3. Creating a product, building a brand, having a funnel, and automating the process through technology in order to systemize a system that makes things work easier.

There are other qualities which lead Brunson to reach peak and optimal performance within his life. He summarizes them with the following, "Surrounding myself with amazing people. It's the energy, it's the ideas, and things from other people; I think that's the big key for me. Having balance. I still workout all the time, I have my family and work time. You can't perform optimally in anything when you're unbalanced. Having a good perspective on what you're trying to do and what you're trying to accomplish; maybe it's goal setting, maybe it's just a vision or something where you really see where you want to go."

Brunson highlighted his three key elements for being successful:

1. Faith in anything is important. Faith in what you do. When I'm going for something, I'm going for something knowing one hundred percent it's going to work. And if I do that, I have perfect faith it's going to work, then I can move mountains to make it happen. The second there is doubt or there is not perfect faith in it, then I get nervous and I can't succeed. Faith in whatever it is you're trying to accomplish, one hundred percent faith that you know it's going to work is one of the most important qualities.

2. People's ability to step in a situation and immediately change yourself. In business or life or whatever it is, how quick you can control your states when you need them to be.

3. Not being concerned if you aren't successful... When you need that, it's tied to your identity. It's hard to get it. Whereas, if you're okay with yourself and you're happy with yourself... It opens up all sorts of doors that otherwise are closed.

Steve Harrison

Publisher of Radio-TV Interview Report and Host of National Publicity Summit

Several years ago, there was a lot of overhead within his business and Steve started tapping into his credit. As time went on, he maxed out the credit line and was on the verge of going bankrupt. Harrison spoke at a seminar and people said his speech was great but they didn't become clients. His brother, Bill, approached him and told him that he had to bring back at least $20,000. "I actually prayed and asked God to help me. I remember being in a ball field and saying that prayer and I didn't get an answer then but what happened was that I got invited to be part of a coaching program and learn more about marketing," said Steve.

As a member in this coaching program, Steve learned how to give a speech in the right manner that would get people interested in his programs. "Once I finished speaking, I had forty people rush to the stage and give me order forms that totaled $67,000. Some of that really did come from improved marketing. I also see it as God really came through for me as well," said Steve.

That was definitely his breakthrough moment. Steve stated, "That was a very transformative experience because that allowed us then to have the cash to keep the company going and then we reinvented ourselves. We just had a service really and I wasn't owning my own expertise. That was the catalyst to say, hey, I'm not just an entrepreneur with a service but I actually am an expert on publicity and one of the things I had offered in that talk was consultations."

After this, Harrison began doing consulting. Then, he began the National Publicity Summit and the Quantum Leap Program. "Ironically, the thing that I was going through to help other people know: How do you claim your expertise? How do you monetize your expertise and how do you promote it? That was the huge thing. Even if somehow that event hadn't succeeded, I think God would have come through for me in some other way. It was just a profound, profound experience," said Steve.

Here are Steve's tactics for reaching peak and optimal performance:

1. Listening first to what people want or what's going on with them. That means listening to your prospects, listening to your employees, listening to your customers, and listening to your own self-talk.
2. Systems, routines, and habits; what is your routine? You want to lose weight. What is your system for actually having that be the case? What is your habit of when are you going to exercise?
3. Love is the number one force that's the most motivating force. As we love and serve other people, we're at our very best.

Steve stressed the importance of loving other people. "You're giving them the benefit of doubt, you're really focused on listening, and you're focused on serving. You don't hear it talked about very much. I do believe it's the least talked about business principle but the most powerful," stated Harrison.

Steve has a very strong commitment and dedication to his clients and customers. "I often say that marketing is love, because when you love somebody, what do you do?

- You listen to them.
- You try to figure out how best to serve them.
- You deliver on what you promised, in fact, you over deliver.
- You're thinking about them before yourself so that's what good marketers do.
- It really begins with helping that person get what they want.

If you really love people, you're going to get much better at persuading them to take action. People will often have doubts or want to procrastinate and you don't serve them by having them say no or procrastinate a decision that would be good for them. In our business, that's one of the ways we're able to market," stated Harrison.

Mike Filsaime

Internet Marketing Expert, Speaker, and Consultant

Mike's breakthrough came from a report that he read from John Reese, *One Man, One Product, One Million Dollars, One Day.* In this report, Reese talked about how he was the first guy to do a million dollar launch within the internet marketing industry. Nobody had ever done over $75,000 before that in a day. However, John did a million dollars in a day.

On August 30th, 2004, Mike read the report and on August 31st, he registered the domain: butterflymarketing.com. "That report inspired me to think big and do what he did simply because he created the roadmap. I said if he can do it, I can do it... I launched my product on January 31st, 2006. It was a year and half later and when I launched Butterfly Marketing, we did a million dollars in five days. We did 1.5 million dollars in 30 days," said Mike.

This was a major accomplishment for Mike and it elevated him to a highly respected level within the industry as an expert. "That had incredible repercussions that went through the industry and through my career after that. The genesis, the seed of that product launch came from reading that report from a guy named John Reese that showed me that if you create something that you believe has a value in this world, there is a recipe; a model that you can follow, that can get people to buy," stated Mike.

Mike's career continued to rise after that point and he "never looked back from that point on."

There are three qualities important to Mike in order to reach success:

1. Having an entrepreneur mindset. Being an entrepreneur means that we don't look at the box that society puts us in. Being an entrepreneur, there are no limits and you don't do things for the money, you do them for the freedom and lifestyle that it gives you; the value that you can put into the world by doing so. Your income is directly proportionate to the amount of value that you give and by the number of people that you affect.
2. Have a way to give back; you want to have some type of philanthropy in your life where you can take what God or the universe has given you and be able to give back to the less fortunate. It is definitely important go give back to certain charities and foundations.

3. You need to be doing something that you're passionate about. Success truly comes from being able to do something that you're passionate about; making sure that you're happy in what you do. Success is not just about money, it's about ultimate happiness in your lifestyle, in your life.

Chapter 12

THE MILLIONAIRE LEGACY

"I don't spend time thinking about a legacy. I just help wherever I can. I love what I'm doing, just love helping people."

—Bob Proctor

A legacy is an imprint in the lives of the people that you impact positively within your lifetime and also for generations to come. When you give to others with a pureness of heart and without any expectation of receiving anything back in return, this will create a ripple effect of love that will be non-stoppable and will continue to spread out to the universe. Subsequently, the inner joy and peace that you receive back from this unselfish act will be substantial. Simply put, when you allow yourself to become open and generous to others, then God, Jesus, and the universe is also generous to you.

Having a huge bank account is only a temporary gain and cannot bring satisfaction and contentment. At times, people may have a tendency to become consumed with the acquisition of wealth and material items. Wealth can give you the life of your dreams and it can also be used to help people in a very positive manner. In order to attain peace, happiness, and contentment, extend kindness and love to others.

According to Brendon Burchard, at the end of our lives, we are going to ask three important questions:

- Did I live?
- Did I love?
- Did I matter?

These are critical questions to think about now so that you don't have any regrets in years to come. Don't allow days, weeks, and months to pass by without taking decisive action. If you let fear or past failure prevent you from pursuing your dreams, you will never be able to realize your true potential.

In your life, your positive accomplishments, giving, and sharing with others can be a strong legacy that will live on for many years. Zig Ziglar was an author, salesman, and motivational speaker who impacted a large number of people throughout his career. When you mention Ziglar's name, no one cares about how much money he had. People care about the positive message and impression that Ziglar left in their lives. As a result, his legacy will live on for many years to come.

For the millionaires presented in this book, their driving force is to help other people with their products, services, and through their support of respected charities. They are not obsessed with making a massive amount of cash. Remarkably, money comes to them just like they are a magnet because they are solving a problem or need while assisting others. Simply put, their motive is a genuine concern for humanity and this is very evident.

Let's look at the legacies of each of the millionaires presented in this book. The following passages are direct quotes from each one of the millionaires.

Bob Proctor

I don't spend a lot of time thinking about a legacy. I spend all my time thinking on how to help somebody, how to help others. I want our company to give a lot away. I have no desire to save it or to grow it; I just see us as an instrument. We build schools in Africa. We do a lot of work with Cynthia Kersey because I like what she's doing, so we support her. I want people to learn what I'm teaching. I love teaching it to people. I want it to go on and on. I don't want it to stop with me. I don't think it will stop with me. I want to create an instrument where we continue this whether I'm here or not, and that's what we do in our company. I've got a great partner in Sandra Gallagher; she's a brilliant lady. A very successful banking attorney until she got mixed into studying this and then this is all she wants to do. She left her law practice to do this and she's really the business brains behind our business. I'm more of the creative guy. I just want to create. I just help wherever I can. I just see myself as an ordinary guy having a great life; loving what I'm doing and just love helping people with it because it's so good.

Brendon Burchard

At the end of all of our lives, when we're gone, I think our only legacy is our message, our example, and our love for other people. I don't think there's anything left. When I think about my father, he's gone. In spirit, he's still in our hearts. In spirit, we feel, still feel and sense, and have memories of him, but what is it we really have memory to? Well, we remember how he loved us. We remember what he said to us. We remember how he lived his life. I think those are the only things people are going to remember? I think my books will always be around and my video's will always be around. All these things will be around after I'm gone. But, when people reflect and remember it; that's the stuff of legacy, is what people reflect on and remember of you after you're gone. I think that is what people will recall and I would hope that I do a good job in sharing a very clear and helpful message with the world. That people continue to look at me as an example of what's possible because that's all I'm trying to be. Just to show, hey, look what I can do; you guys can do this. Just trying to live a good life of virtue along the way and avoid all the vices and the simple reasonings in which we can become more apathetic or distraught, or frustrated, or angry, or judgmental human beings. Then, at the end of the day, I think the only legacy that really matters; the only people who are going to remember you, one or two generations away, unless you get your name on a building and even then, they will ask, who's that guy? The only real tangible material lasting legacy is love.

Mark Victor Hansen

Legacy… I don't spend much time there because I'm going to live to be 127 with options for renewal. Most people would say your legacy is the biggest book series. Well, that's nice, but that's not it. I will refinance America. I will reenergize the world with electric energy by creating it alternatively and innovatively. Colonel Sanders didn't even start until after retirement age and there are a lot of people that hit that category. So I think we're in a very exalted, exciting period. Dickens line everybody's got memorized, "It's the best of times, it's the worst of times."

To watch normal media and believe it every day; it's all slated against you. It's the best of times!

Sean D. Tucker

A legacy is who that person is. A legacy is all of it, whether you're ethical. It's who you've touched in your life. Did I empower people? Was a person better off interacting with me than before they interacted with me? I want them to be better off. Some museums want my airplane. They say, "This is your legacy to have your airplane hanging in the museum." I'm inducted into the National Aviation Hall of Fame. To me, that's not a legacy. What that is: a lifetime achievement award, but that's not the legacy. A legacy is: Did I leave the world a better place? Is the world that much brighter because I was in it? Is the world that much more empowered because I was in it? Did I leave it a better place? I want to leave the world a better place and the question is if somebody mentions a name, did I leave the world more colorful? Did I leave the world more important? Did I leave the world more joy? And if they said yes, I've fulfilled on my destiny as a human being.

James Malinchak

My legacy is: I'm very crystal clear about what I do; I help a lot of folks who truthfully don't really know how to make money with their business because we've never really been taught that. We've never been taught that in school. A lot of people are business owners but they're not entrepreneurs. A lot of people don't really know how to run a profitable business. It's not about ROI, it's about net income, and how much you keep. A lot of people don't know that debt is not a good way to live and I'm very clear when I'm helping someone create plans. We're making these plans and marketing moves to bring them net income.

I'm very clear what my unique talent is. Everybody has a strong unique talent that they're really good at. There is no bigger thrill for me than when I see the twinkle in somebody's eye in my seminar or whether I'm doing a consulting for them. When they see the plan, the actual real life plan I put together for them, and I see that twinkle and I see the belief. They change how they're talking. I see their spirit rise and they know they can do it and then they go out and they actually do it. They keep serving and doing what they love to do: teaching, delivering great value, their products, their services, but now they're actually making great net income while doing all that great stuff. There is no bigger thrill for me because I know that now they're going to get out of debt. They're going to take care of their aging parents. They're going to pay for their kids to go to school. They're going to pay off that house. They are not going to get foreclosed on if they have a business or a home. They're going to be able to make their car payments. They're not going to stress which means some of them aren't going to have marriage problems because a lot of marriages end in divorce because of financial reasons, not because of infidelity.

I want people to say, "I went to Malinchak and he helped me. He truly cared about me because he made sure that my family was taken care of with the way we structured our business." I don't need it written up in a newspaper. I don't need any of that stuff.

I have a room. It's called an appreciation room and I have hundreds, probably thousands of thank you cards and notes from people that I've helped. I save all of them, every single one of them, and I write back to every single one of them. Every person that ever writes me, I write back to them and I saved all these because that's what it's about. And when I'm having a bad day and I want to kind of go "woe is me," I look at these notes and cards. That gets me up off the ground and keeps me going.

Russell Brunson

We're publishing some things in a lot of different industries. We're in this process now of transitioning our business model into something that's kind of more of a legacy thing for me that will withstand the test of time. We're taking Dotcom Secrets, which is a business that most people would know is our internet marketing company, and using that as a place to show the results of what's happening.

We're focusing a lot in our other companies like getting good results and showing that. We're re-launching one of our newsletters that is going to be showing test results; here's what's working, here's what's not working, and trying just to make people better marketers. We've got two software products we're rolling out. In the future, we can have hundreds of thousands of people using it. We are showing how we're using these tools in our business.

We do this business. We aren't just talking about it. We're doing it. You can see it in our twelve other companies. Dotcom Secrets is where we're sharing results of what's happening, here is the software that drives us, and we're trying to educate everybody else on how to use it. That's our goal. Focusing a lot on working with big companies and helping them get more traffic and more sales; that's the legacy we want. Just really being able to be an amplifier for businesses, take whatever they've got, and help them to ramp it up very quickly.

My personal life… A couple years ago my identity was so tied to my business and now it's not. We're trying to get less and less because that's not as important to me anymore. My legacy personally is the core group of people that I consider friends. I always have been and always will be a good friend. For my family, that I'll be an amazing dad and a husband. That's really the most important thing to me. I think that the longer I've been doing this, the less important the money and the business part of it is and more important is the relationships. You really understand who's there with you through the thick and thin, who you can trust, building those relationships, and hopefully being the kind of friend to them that I would want them to be to me. That's my personal legacy.

Steve Harrison

I want to have a company that's known worldwide for helping; helping people claim their expertise, share it with the world, have a lot of fun, and make really good money doing it. There is a personal legacy. There is a phrase I heard once, "To glorify God and enjoy Him forever." I'm not sure that it necessarily meets the criteria of a legacy but it's certainly a driving force as a Christian; that I might just use my gifts and talents to serve the Lord. That can take a lot of different manifestations.

Mike Filsaime

My legacy is not changeable, if it's something that can't be quantified. For me, my legacy is just knowing that I have the opportunity to inspire, enact, and enable lots of people to go from a regular mindset to an entrepreneur mindset; a millionaire mindset. I can leave the millionaire legacy behind in the works and the deeds that I do on a day-to-day basis. And

I know the story of the Keith Wellman, of the Alex Jeffreys. I know how Russell Brunson and I inspired each other. I know the people like Ken Spano, Jane Sharenko, the people that came up to me and said, "I'm in this business because of you. It was your product." Josh Bartlett reading the Butterfly Marketing manuscripts and knowing what a guy like Josh Bartlett was able to do and Alex Jeffreys, how many people he's helped in his coaching programs. How many businesses were helped because of Josh Bartlett's easy video player or easy video suite and how it's helped them and their business. So, my legacy, I don't need to quantify it. I just want to know that if I continue doing what I'm doing, I'm changing the world for the better and that's my legacy. I don't need a statue.

Each millionaire has their own unique legacy that is important to them. What type of legacy do you want for your life? This is an important question that you should ask yourself. Remember that acts of kindness, love, and sharing with other people will resonate with them for many years to come.

Give openly and with the right intention that comes from the heart. The joy and inner satisfaction that you receive from giving is tremendous. When you look back years from now, you will think about the times that you shared with others and extended unconditional love to them; this will be your legacy.

MILLIONAIRE BIOGRAPHIES

Bob Proctor

To millions of people across the globe, the name Bob Proctor is synonymous with success. Long before his role in the movie *The Secret* sent him into the realm of superstardom, he was already a legendary figure in the world of personal development. His insights, inspiration, ideas, systems, and strategies are the dimes on which countless lives have spun — the sparks that have ignited career transformations, personal epiphanies, inner awakenings, and the creation of million-dollar fortunes the world over.

Bob is the heir to the legacy of the modern science of success that began with the financier and philanthropist Andrew Carnegie. Carnegie's great challenge to the young reporter Napoleon Hill to discern a formula for success fueled Hill's creation of the renowned book *Think and Grow Rich*. Upon discovering this book at the age of 26, Bob's life changed in an instant, leading him on his own quest for the secrets of success.

That quest led him to Earl Nightingale, the famed "Dean of Personal Development" who soon became Bob's colleague and mentor. Today, Bob continues to build upon and spread the remarkable teachings of these three giants.

As a speaker, author, consultant, coach, and mentor, Bob Proctor works with business entities and individuals around the world, instilling within them not only the mental foundations of success and the motivation to achieve, but also the actionable strategies that will empower them to grow, improve, and thrive in today's ever-changing world. Through the Proctor Gallagher Institute, Bob, Sandy Gallagher, and their team teach the principles, strategies and fundamentals that help people and organizations create the results they want in life… results that STICK.

For more information, please visit:

http://www.proctorgallagherinstitute.com

Brendon Burchard

Brendon Burchard is a #1 *New York Times* bestselling author whose books include: *Life's Golden Ticket, The Millionaire Messenger, The Charge: Activating the 10 Human Drives that Make You Feel Alive,* and *The Motivation Manifesto.* After surviving a car accident at the age of 19, Brendon Burchard received what he calls "life's golden ticket," a second chance. Since then, he has dedicated his life to helping others find their charge and share their voice with the world.

He is the founder of High Performance Academy, the legendary personal development program for achievers, and Experts Academy, the world's most comprehensive marketing training for authors, speakers, life coaches, and online thought leaders. For these works, Larry King named him "one of the top motivation and marketing trainers in the world."

Brendon's books have been #1 *New York Times,* #1 *Wall Street Journal,* #1 *USA Today,* #1 Amazon.com, and #1 Barnes and Noble bestsellers. He is regularly seen on public television and has appeared on Larry King, Anderson Cooper, ABC World News, CBS News, Oprah and Friends, NPR stations, The Wall Street Journal TV, and other popular outlets like SUCCESS Magazine, Inc.com, Forbes.com, FastCompany.com, and *The Huffington Post.*

Though best known as a motivational speaker and high performance trainer, Brendon is on speed dial as a marketing advisor to the world's leading companies and celebrities. His online marketing campaigns continue to set worldwide records. He has launched 12 online promotions in a row that crossed $1,000,000 in sales in less than seven days each, with five of those campaigns crossing $2,000,000 and two crossing $4,000,000.

For more information, please visit:

http://brendonburchard.com
http://highperformanceacademy.com
http://www.expertsacademy.com
http://worldsgreatestspeakertraining.com

Mark Victor Hansen

Mark Victor Hansen is a world-renowned authority in the field of self-development and business building for kids and adults. The best-selling author of the *Chicken Soup for the Soul* and *One Minute Millionaire* series, founder of the RichestKidsAcademy.com and winner of the prestigious Horatio Alger Award, he has been on thousands of radio and TV shows, and is the host of the infomercial series, The Hansen Report, seen daily by millions worldwide.

Hansen is the prolific author of more than three hundred books, including fifty-nine New York Times number one bestsellers. Hansen's books have been published in more than forty-four languages. He loves inspiring individuals to write and create and publish their own books at his website, wealthywriterswisdom.com.

Hansen's popularity as an international inspirational speaker and seminar leader is exemplified by an impressive list of more than five thousand talks to over five million people.

An avid outdoorsman, Hansen has climbed some of the world's highest mountains: Whitney, Fuji, Mach Picchu, etc. He has visited and taken in 78 countries, with the goal to do all 228 countries. He has traveled in excess of five million miles. He is a resident of Newport Beach, California, where he lives with his soul mate, Crystal. They have five adult children and three grandchildren.

Hansen also has deep interests and investments in alternative green/ clean energy. He is working zealously to create a sustainable economy and ecology.

For more information, please visit:

http://markvictorhansen.com

Sean D. Tucker

Sean D. Tucker is more than a remarkable aviator and industry leading aerobatic pilot. He's celebrated by his peers, adored by his fans and recognized by Smithsonian National Air and Space Museum as a Living Legend of Flight.

With a full-throttle attitude, he shares his passion for aviation, inspiring others to pursue their dreams, conquer their fears and refine their skills. His enthusiasm is contagious. It's evident in his ground-breaking, one-of-a-kind aerobatic maneuvers that make millions of jaws drop each year. Tucker's life is marked by a search for excellence and a drive to overcome. What started as a quest to conquer a fear of flying has evolved into the art of precision, performance and perfected skill.

The level of professionalism and discipline in Tucker's airshows is no coincidence. He practices his air show routine three times every day. To endure the extreme physical demands of each routine, Tucker maintains a rigorous physical training schedule, working out more than 340 days per year.

Tucker has been thrilling air show audiences since he first took to the skies as an aerobatic pilot in 1976. Since then, he has won dozens of aerobatic competitions, flown more than 1,225 performances at nearly 500 airshows in front of more than 125 million fans.

Tucker is the founder and president of the California-based, non-profit Every Kid Can Fly that facilitates transformative life experiences in education and aviation for at-risk and underprivileged teenagers. Every Kid Can Fly empowers teens to cultivate skills necessary to thrive in a modern world, inspires teens to pursue education and careers in

STEM programs and recalibrates teens' perceptions of what they are capable of achieving.

In 2013, the Experimental Aircraft Association named Tucker as the chairman of aviation's flagship program to introduce children to flight, Young Eagles. Tucker has assumed the responsibility with great commitment, engaging kids in aviation and recognizing the more than 45,000 volunteer pilots who have flown approximately 1.9 million Young Eagles since the program began.

For more information, please visit:

http://teamoracle.com
http://poweraerobatics.com
http://everykidcanfly.org
http://www.youngeagles.org

James Malinchak

You may have never heard of James Malinchak, but he is "One of the Most Requested Business & Motivational Speakers in the World" and has delivered over 2,000 presentations for business groups, corporations, colleges, universities and youth organizations worldwide for audiences ranging from 20 to 6,000 and has done so without being famous, any advanced academic degrees and without any speaker designations from any speaker associations. He was Twice Named "College Speaker of the Year!"

From a small Pennsylvania steel-mill town, to self-made millionaire motivational speaker! James Malinchak is a true American Success Story who is 1 of ONLY 7 people in the world featured on the Hit Primetime Reality ABC TV Show, *"SECRET MILLIONAIRE!"* James is the ONLY Public Speaker Trainer in the world featured on "Secret Millionaire," and gave away $100,000+ of his own money on the show. An important part of James Malinchak's life is to give-back to those less fortunate, with numerous personal five-digit donations and raising over $500,000 for kid's charities in the past 18 months alone.

James is known worldwide as "Big Money Speaker®" & is recognized as "The World's #1 Big Money Speaker® Trainer & Coach" for anyone who wants to Get Highly Paid As a Speaker. James has written 12 books...including co-authoring the BEST-SELLER, *Chicken Soup for the College Soul.* He was named Marketer of the Year by *Marketing Guru's Dan Kennedy & Bill Glazer* and Was Named "Top 40 Business People Under Age 40 in Las Vegas." James is one of the most in-demand, highest paid business marketing coaches in the world, with fees ranging from $15,000 – $100,000.

For more information, please visit:
http://malinchak.com
http://bigmoneyspeaker.com
http://collegespeakingsuccessbootcamp.com

Russell Brunson

Russell Brunson started his first online business when he was in college and started selling potato gun DVDs. This little hobby became his obsession and he started selling all sorts of things online. He became a student of marketing.

In high school, Russell was a state champion at 140 lbs, and became an All-American in his senior year when Russell took 2nd place in the country at high school nationals. He then wrestled a year at BYU before they dropped their program, and then he transferred to Boise State and wrestled in his last 4 years there at 165 lbs. Wrestling is really where Brunson found himself, and he doesn't think there's a day that goes by that he doesn't miss being in a wrestling room. (That's probably why Russell is doing Jiu Jitsu now)

When Russell got done wrestling, he shifted his focus towards his new business. In his senior year, he had made about $250,000... and within a year of graduation, he had made his millionth dollar selling little products that he created. Brunson collects junk mail. When he listens to the radio or watches TV, he is usually watching for the commercials and will fast forward through a show to watch a commercial because that is REAL entertainment for him. He loves marketing and sales. It was so exciting that he wanted to share it with the world. He started writing about what he was doing. He got invited to speak at seminars all around the world, and he launched his blog, DotComSecrets, to show people the secrets that he learned about how to start, grow, and promote a business online.

Brunson had the opportunity of speaking at Tony Robbin's "Business Mastery Seminar in Fiji." While he was going to college, he met his beautiful wife Collette, and they have been married for over 10 years.

For more information, please visit:

http://www.dotcomsecrets.com

Steve Harrison

Steve Harrison is a dream maker. If you are willing to dream big and want to live your dream, Steve can show you the way to create unparalleled success in your life. Since 1987, he's been consulting and advising authors and entrepreneurs on how to promote their books, products, and services.

He's been responsible for getting more than 15,000 people – including over 12,000 authors – booked on radio and TV talk shows -- which is more than any PR firm on the planet!

As publisher of *Radio-TV Interview Report (RTIR)*, he's helped launch such bestselling books as *Chicken Soup for the Soul, Rich Dad Poor Dad, The Worst Case Scenario* series, and the *Dummies* series, just to name a few.

He is the creator of the Quantum Leap program for authors. He also presents the *National Publicity Summit* in New York, where he opens his personal Rolodex and gives 100 publicity-seeking authors and entrepreneurs the once-in-a-lifetime chance to meet face-to-face with producers, editors, and journalists, from shows like *Good Morning America, Time Magazine, Family Circle, Live with Kelly & Michael, ABC's 20/20, Dateline NBC*, CNN, Fox News, and more than 100 others.

He is the co-creator of the Best Seller Blueprint with Jack Canfield.

For more information, please visit:

http://www.rtir.com
http://www.nationalpublicitysummit.com
http://www.bestsellerblueprint.com

Mike Filsaime

Mike Filsaime is an Online Entrepreneur and has been described as the **"Michael Jordan of Internet Marketing"** because of the expertise and knowledge he has shared over the years as an educator of innovative and cutting edge strategies.

Mike is also an author, software developer, renowned speaker, and business consultant and runs one of the best and largest Closed-Door Master Minds in Internet Marketing.

Mike regularly travels with other self-made millionaires raising money for charities as he does extreme adventures like Jumping out of planes at 30,000 feet, zero gravity dives, driving the Baja, and trips to the remote parts of Haiti that you can only get to by small planes. His ventures have raised over $100,000 for different charities.

Mike Filsaime was the General Manager of one of the nation's largest auto dealers. 14 years in the auto business along with his education at the New York Institute of Technology in Computer Science and Business Administration has allowed Mike to understand Marketing, Advertising, Sales, Customer Service, long term Business Principles, and how to use the Internet to leverage these items to new successes.

Many of the people Mike has helped with Internet marketing have gone on to have incredible success in a very short amount of time after working with him. Many of them are now Internet millionaires working full-time with their new businesses. Mike Filsaime is known as a leader in the industry. Mike has been fortunate to spend personal time with people such as Mark Victor Hansen, Dr. Joe Vitale, Tony Robbins, and Oren Klaff. He has even given marketing advice to the Director of films at Robbins Research International as well as Trump University as well as offered personal one-on-one advice on Internet Marketing to Tony Robbins.

For more information, please visit:

http://mikefilsaime.com

THE HEART OF A MILLIONAIRE
BIOGRAPHIES

Chesley B. "Sully" Sullenberger, III

Chesley B. "Sully" Sullenberger, III has been dedicated to the pursuit of safety for his entire adult life. While he is best known for serving as Captain during what has been dubbed the "Miracle on the Hudson," Sullenberger is an aviation safety expert and accident investigator, serves as a CBS News Aviation and Safety Expert, and is the founder and chief executive officer of Safety Reliability Methods, Inc., a company dedicated to management, safety, performance, and reliability consulting.

Born and raised in Denison, Texas, Sullenberger pursued his childhood love of aviation at the United States Air Force Academy. Upon graduation from the Academy, Sullenberger served as a fighter pilot for the United States Air Force from 1975 to 1980. He advanced to become a flight leader and a training officer, attaining the rank of captain. During his active duty, he was stationed in North America and Europe. After serving in the Air Force, Sullenberger became an airline pilot with Pacific Southwest Airlines, later acquired by US Airways, until his retirement in March 2010.

After logging more than 20,000 hours of flight time Sullenberger became internationally renowned on January 15, 2009 when he and his crew safely guided US Airways Flight 1549 to an emergency water landing in New York City's frigid Hudson River. The Airbus A320's two engines had lost thrust following a bird strike.

Since his retirement from US Airways, Sullenberger served as co-chairman until 2013 of the EAA Young Eagles — a program that inspires and educates youth about aviation. He has become the *New York Times* best-selling author of "*Highest Duty: My Search for What Really Matters*" and also wrote "*Making a Difference: Stories of Vision and Courage from America's Leaders.*" He is an international lecturer and keynote speaker at educational institutions, corporations and non-profit organizations about the importance of aviation and patient safety, crisis management, life-long preparation, leadership, and living a life of integrity.

For more information, please visit:

http://sullysullenberger.com

Karolyn Grimes

At the tender age of 4, Karolyn Grimes began memorizing lines and acting in the fantasy world of cinema. She worked with film legends John Wayne, Cary Grant, Bing Crosby, Loretta Young, Fred MacMurray, Betty Grable, Danny Kaye and, of course, Jimmy Stewart. She already had appeared in four films when the part of Zuzu came along. It was just another small part, but one that has made an indelible imprint on the American consciousness.

Karolyn's life has not always been wonderful. In fact, tragedy beset her early and often. Her Hollywood career ended in her teens when her mother died from early-onset Alzheimer's disease and her father was killed in an automobile accident. An only child, Karolyn was sent by the court to live in tiny Osceola, Mo. Living in a less than desirable home, she found support from the townspeople, and, through their love and encouragement, Karolyn decided to get an education and became a medical technician.

She eventually married and had two little girls. The marriage ended in divorce, and two years later her girls' father was killed in a hunting accident. Karolyn then married a man who had three children. They had two more together, so Karolyn raised a family of seven children. Her son committed suicide at age 18, and Karolyn describes this time in her life as the most devastating. As she climbed out of that despair, her husband of 25 years died from lung cancer.

At the time, the rebirth of interest in "It's a Wonderful Life" had begun, and Karolyn soon found a new life's focus. She moved to the Seattle area from Missouri and serves as the unofficial ambassador for the film, traveling the world and speaking at screenings, benefits, conventions and other venues. Her sparkling personality and her courageous story allows her audiences to feel good about themselves and their lives, no matter the hardship.

For more information, please visit:

http://www.zuzu.net

Julie Clark

Julie Clark is a retired Northwest Airlines Captain and aerobatic pilot who logged more than 32,000 accident-free hours in the air. She has been a pilot for more than 42 years.

There was never a doubt that Julie Clark was born to fly. While most 8 year old girls were playing with dolls, Julie was building models of airplanes and reading about flying. Her father, Captain Ernie Clark, Chief Pilot for Pacific Airlines, got her "interested in flying" and he would take her along "on airline flights in the DC-3 or F-27."

Julie spent her college book money on flying lessons. After college, years of working two and three jobs and taking virtually any flying job to build time and higher ratings, Julie's major break came in 1976 when Golden West Airlines, a West Coast commuter airline, hired her to fly DeHavilland Twin Otters. The first, and only, woman ever to fly for Golden West, Julie flew mail at night and passengers until noon, in her continuing effort to build time. In 1977, when Hughes Airwest (formerly Pacific Airlines) hired Julie, she became one of the first women to fly for a major airline and it started what has become a storybook career. Hughes Airwest became Republic Airlines and is now Northwest Airlines. Julie became a Captain for Northwest Airlines in 1984. After a long and enjoyable career with the airlines, Julie retired from Northwest Airlines in 2004.

Clark has received numerous awards. In March of 2002, Julie received perhaps her highest honor with induction into the Women in Aviation Pioneer Hall of Fame of Women in Aviation, International.

It was announced that Tempest and Electroair are going to jointly support the Julie Clark Air Shows. "I'm really excited about our partnership with Tempest and Electroair," said Julie Clark. "After many years of flying my original Beechcraft T-34 in air shows (35+ years),

I'm real excited about this new adventure, and flying with the state-of-the-art modern electronic ignition by Electroair coupled with Tempest high-energy spark plugs. I think this will definitely add "spark" to my airshow performance!"

Julie is one of the few air show greats to be featured in a biography; her amazing story is told in *NOTHING STOOD IN HER WAY, Julie Clark,* which was the first such biography published by Women in Aviation, International and tells of the amazing strengths and perseverance of this remarkable air show star.

For more information, please visit:

http://julieclarkairshows.com

ABOUT THE AUTHOR

Thomas P. Curran

Thomas P. Curran graduated with a Bachelor of Arts degree in psychology from DePaul University in Chicago, Illinois. He was a member of the National Honor Society in Psychology and co-authored a media-based stress management intervention research project which was published in the *Journal of Community Psychology*.

He entered the field of radio and worked as an on-air personality, executive producer, and talk show host. His unique ability to convey valuable information to the listeners while keeping them stimulated and actively engaged is truly remarkable.

As a consultant, he utilizes an education based marketing approach with an emphasis on audio and video. Thomas is able to assist his clients in developing strategic marketing plans, implementing effective strategies to encourage peak performance from employees, launching systematic frameworks for increasing customers and revenue, and teaching clients how to utilize effective time management skills.

Thomas is a certified trainer and has developed training curriculums and performance evaluations. He incorporates a scenario based training methodology to assist teams in maximizing their skills.

As a speaker and seminar leader, his skill in helping individuals develop a clearly defined plan for success, experience a positive emotional awakening, and prioritize their goals, dreams, and aspirations has distinguished him as the foremost expert within the area. His presentations are energetic and motivating.

With a strong passion for aviation, Thomas is an active member of the Experimental Aircraft Association (EAA) and the Aircraft Owners and Pilots Association (AOPA).

Meet Thomas and receive additional training and resources at:

http://www.thomaspcurran.com

ACKNOWLEDGMENTS
Thomas P. Curran

The unconditional love received from Grandma Elizabeth, Mom, and Heather provided the inspiration for this book...

I have to start by acknowledging Mike Filsaime who played a major role in this entire project. Mike, through your support, kindness, and friendship, I am able to live my passion and dream. I am very thankful and blessed to call you my friend.

Before I continue, I would like to thank all of the millionaires who agreed to be interviewed for this book: Bob Proctor, Brendon Burchard, Mark Victor Hansen, Sean D. Tucker, James Malinchak, Russell Brunson, Steve Harrison, and Mike Filsaime. In addition, I also want to personally thank Captain Chesley "Sully" Sullenberger, Karolyn Grimes, and Captain Julie Clark. It is a great honor and privilege to include all of these amazing individuals within this book.

I want to thank the entire team at Morgan James Publishing. I want to extend my deepest appreciation to David Hancock and Rick Frishman who were responsible for ensuring that this book was published and released. David and Rick, you are allowing me the opportunity of sharing my message with the world and living my dream. I am very happy to be a member of the Morgan James Family.

For my Grandma Elizabeth, Mom, Dad, Uncle Bob, and Uncle Mike who all played an important role in my life in a very positive direction. Grandma Elizabeth raised me as one of her own children and taught me the importance of having respect for others and maintaining a strong faith in Jesus and admiration for Mother Mary. I am thankful for treasured memories and the support that I received from my Dad, Uncle Bob, and Uncle Mike. For my dad and his wife, there is a special recognition. Uncle Bob, I enjoyed our countless trips up to Oshkosh, Wisconsin every summer to attend the annual Experimental Aircraft Association (EAA) airshow and fly in, AirVenture.

Mom supported me in all areas of my life with an open heart of love and understanding. For Rich, you went after your dream of becoming a chef and managing your own restaurant. Your support and love for mom is always remembered. Heather, you supported and encouraged me through countless hours of interviews, research, writing, editing, proofreading, and video production. I am very thankful for your support and unconditional love.

For my sister Lori, your beautiful love for Mom and your Dad is held deep within their souls. You pursued your dream of having your own business and you are extending love on a daily basis to your clients… I know that Mom and your Dad are very proud of you. For my brother Jim, your love for Mom is forever, transcends this earthly plane, and radiates throughout heaven.

I want to acknowledge Sean D. Tucker who is a phenomenal aerobatic pilot. Sean, you are able to live your passion on a daily basis and extend your kindness, generosity, and love to your family, friends, spectators, and employees. As Chairman of the Young Eagles Program, I am confident that you will continue to guide the program in a positive direction while inspiring children and teens to pursue their goals in life. Sean, you are a definite inspiration to everyone who has the opportunity of enjoying your aerial routine, *Sky Dance*, and for anyone who is able to meet with you. I am honored to call you my EAA brother and friend.

For any of my friends who are not specifically mentioned by name, I want you to know that I am thankful for your support and friendship. I know that my Mom is happy for the thoughtfulness and love that you graciously extended to me.

For a very dear friend, Mary Jean, who pushed me and motivated me to maintain strength for life even though challenging obstacles were thrown in my path. Mary Jean, I hold this within my heart and my gratitude is immense for what you have done for me and your continued support.

This book would not be possible without the blessing of Jesus, Mother Mary, and St. Jude...

"Visit with your family and friends. Cherish the time with them while they are here are on Earth because time is so short..."

—Quote inspired by Mercy
Mitera Se Agapo

THE ROAD TO A MILLION DOLLARS: 10 AREAS FOR WEALTH CREATION

This section will provide information on creating a million dollars from products and services you can market and sell.

There are several income opportunities in which you can generate substantial revenue. Speakers, seminar leaders, life coaches, authors, consultants, and experts are sharing their knowledge with others and being paid to do it. When you have a special expertise, you will discover that you are in high demand and people will want to become your client or student so that they can learn from you.

You will be shown how to make $100,000 in each of the following ten areas for wealth creation. If you add them up, they equal one million dollars. Realize that there are some individuals who are making six or seven figures a year by specializing in only one of the business opportunities listed below. You may want to begin with one of the products or services and get that mastered first before you start venturing into other fields. In time, you can expand even further.

Generally, millionaires have multiple streams of income. When you become creative, some of the wealth creation tactics listed below build off each other and can be used as an opportunity for your current clients to get more in depth training from you.

Disclaimer: The following examples are provided for educational purposes ONLY and there is NO guarantee of making any money. This is determined by your motivation, knowledge, and willingness to take action. Any financial numbers referenced here are simply estimates or projections, and should not be considered exact, actual, or as a promise of potential earnings. All numbers are illustrative only.

10 Areas for Wealth Creation

1. Seminars
2. Life Coaching, Business Coaching, and Consulting
3. Audio Program
4. DVD Program
5. Master Mind Mentoring Program
6. Subscription / Membership Site
7. Speaker
8. Online Training Course
9. Books and eBooks
10. Workshops

1. Seminars

The amount of money that can be made from hosting a seminar is surprising to a number of people. This is one area that gives you the opportunity of sharing your expertise with your students. When you host your seminar, you can also invite other experts to speak at your event.

If you host 4 events during the year
and get 25 students at each event:

Cost per attendee: $1,000
Event #1: 25 Students x (times) $1,000 = $25,000
Event #2: 25 Students x (times) $1,000 = $25,000
Event #3: 25 Students x (times) $1,000 = $25,000
Event #4: 25 Students x (times) $1,000 = $25,000
Total Amount = $100,000

** The revenue generated from the above events can be increased even further. At each event, you offer the attendees the opportunity of getting one-on-one coaching directly from you for either $1,500 or $2,000 per month. As a result, you will create a consistent source of revenue on a monthly basis.

2. Life Coaching, Business Coaching, and Consulting

Within the coaching and consulting industry, the amount of money that experts generate can vary greatly. Let's assume that you are charging $2,000 a month for each of your coaching clients. Then, all you need is 5 Coaching Clients per month in order to generate $120,000 per year.

Cost per coaching client: $2,000 per month
5 Coaching Clients per Month
5 people x (times) $2,000 = $10,000 / month
$10,000 / month x (times) 12 months = $120,000

If you charged $1,000 per month for each client, you would only need 9 clients each month in order to generate $108,000 for the year.

3. Audio Program

An audio program is an opportunity for you to share your information with your students. You could record a training course on six CDs or provide a 30 day coaching program. This can be offered in one of the following formats: CDs, downloadable mp3 files from your website, or placed on a flash drive.

Cost per audio program: $197.00
Sell 43 per Month
43 audio programs x (times) $197 = $8,471 / month
$8,471 / month x (times) 12 months = $101,652

4. DVD Program

Videotape a training segment for your clients. If you don't want to appear on camera, you can use your voice and screen recording software to produce a video that can be viewed over the internet or put on a DVD.

Cost per DVD program: $97.00
Sell 86 per Month
86 DVD programs x (times) $97.00 = $8,342 / month
$8,342 / month x (times) 12 months = $100,104

5. Master Mind Mentoring Program

A master mind mentoring program allows you the opportunity of bringing together like-minded people who want to help each other. You act as the coordinator and leader to encourage participation from all members. In addition, you can also provide your tips and strategies with the group.

Cost per Master Mind Client: $1,000 per month
9 Clients per Month
9 people x (times) $1,000 = $9,000 / month
$9,000 / month x (times) 12 months = $108,000

6. Subscription / Membership Site

Your students can log into a membership site to learn strategies, access interviews, and get training material.

Cost per member: $67.00 per month
125 Students per Month
125 people x (times) $67.00 = $8,375 / month
$8,375 / month x (times) 12 months = $100,500

7. Speaker

Companies, organizations, colleges, and universities pay people to give keynote speeches. This area can generate substantial wealth. There are some speakers averaging $5,000 to $20,000 or more per speech.

Cost per speech: $5,000
2 per Month
2 keynote speeches x (times) $5,000 = $10,000 / month
$10,000 / month x (times) 12 months = $120,000

8. Online Training Course

Develop your own online training course that can be accessed by your students from your website.

Cost per online course: $497
17 students sign up per month
17 people x (times) $497 = $8,449
$8,449 / month x (times) 12 months = $101,388

9. Books and eBooks

Write your own book and you can self-publish. Some people will utilize a print-on-demand service in which your book is only printed when there is a paid order. You can also sell online and make your information available in eBook format.

Cost per book: $27
310 sold per month
310 books x (times) $27 = $8,370
$8,370 / month x (times) 12 months = $100,440

10. Workshops

One or two day workshops provide a great opportunity to share your knowledge while inspiring your students. If you conduct a workshop, you only need 34 people to register every month in order to generate over $100,000 for the year.

Cost per attendee: $247
34 students attend your monthly workshop
34 people x (times) $247 = $8,398
$8,398 / month x (times) 12 months = $100,776

** The revenue generated from the above workshops can be increased even further. At each event, you offer the attendees the opportunity of getting one-on-one coaching directly from you for $1,000 per month.

MILLIONAIRE LEGACY™
MINDSET ASSESSMENT

The Millionaire Legacy™ Mindset Assessment is a leadership and personality assessment that will determine how your mindset compares to millionaires.

After you complete the assessment, you will be provided with instructions to score your results and generate a percentage for each area being evaluated. At that point, you will know which areas need to be enhanced or improved so that you can model after highly successful millionaires. Realize that you have total choice and power to shift your thinking in a positive manner so that you are closely aligned with the same thought process which is used by affluent individuals.

The Millionaire Legacy™ Mindset Assessment may not be copied or duplicated without the consent of the author. Copies of this assessment may be purchased for your company, organization, or school upon request from the author. Please visit MillionaireLegacy.com.

Disclaimer:

The following assessment is intended for educational purposes only and should not be understood to constitute any type of diagnosis or healthcare recommendation. The mindset assessment, report, and evaluation of results are not intended to replace, nor a substitute in any way for a formal psychiatric or psychological evaluation. For a diagnosis, contact a licensed mental health or medical health care professional. The author, publisher or any of the individuals featured throughout this book shall have no liability for claims by, or damages of any kind whatsoever to, any person for a decision or action taken in reliance on the information contained in the assessment, report, or evaluation of results. Such damages include, without limitation, direct, indirect, special, incidental or consequential damages.

Your use of the assessment, report, and evaluation of results constitutes your agreement to the provisions of this disclaimer.

Answer the following questions with complete honesty for the most accurate result. Please choose the one answer which best represents your response to each situation which is presented.

1. You are asked to become project manager and lead a team that will design and release a brand new product to the market.
   a. This idea scares me and I will have to decline the offer.
   b. There are a lot of problems that can arise with this project and I know it won't work.
   c. This can be very challenging but I am going to do my research to ensure a positive outcome.
   d. I am confident that I can lead the team, develop a great product, and customers will want to purchase it.

2. You have to develop a training curriculum for new employees based upon your knowledge and background.
   a. I am terrified about doing this.
   b. My training modules will be ineffective as a training method for new employees.
   c. I am going to research other training programs within my industry, outline my expertise in a clear manner, and develop the training program.
   d. I have valuable knowledge to share with new employees and my training curriculum will benefit them greatly.

3. You just won millions of dollars in the lottery. How do you proceed?
   a. I am very worried. How am I going to save and spend this large amount of money?
   b. I don't know how to invest money. I know that I will lose it.

    c.   I will start doing my research. I will find financial planners and accountants who can advise me on investing the money and spending it wisely.

    d.   I am very happy and sure that I can make the money grow even bigger.

4.   You are asked to make your very first appearance as a guest on a radio show to discuss a hobby that you have been actively involved in since childhood. As a result, you have extensive knowledge of your hobby and your friends consider you an expert within this area.

    a.   I am apprehensive at the thought of being on the radio and having all those people hear me. I will decline the request.

    b.   I don't know what to say and the listeners won't learn anything from me.

    c.   This is a great opportunity. I am going to make an outline ahead of time with the key points that I want to share with the radio host and listeners.

    d.   I am very excited about sharing my knowledge with a large amount of people who can benefit greatly from my expertise.

5.   You are asked to drive a friend to another city that you are unfamiliar with. You can't use your cell phone or GPS to get you there.

    a.   I am petrified about doing this.

    b.   There is no way that I will be able to find this location. I am going to tell my friend to find someone else.

    c.   I am going to get creative and find other methods to plan my route including maps and the internet.

    d.   After my research is completed, I am positive that I can get my friend to their destination.

6. Your boss asks you to order 10 personalized plaques for an upcoming awards ceremony within the next couple weeks. You have to find a company that specializes in this area, get the plaques produced, and ensure that each person's name is printed correctly on their plaque.

    a.   I am frightened at the thought of not being able to find a company to produce the plaques in time for the ceremony.

    b.   I know that I won't be able to find a company to produce high quality plaques.

    c.   I will immediately begin to research companies that specialize in this area and call each company until I find one that can complete this project.

    d.   I am confident that I will find a great company to produce the plaques for the awards ceremony.

7. Your best friend of 20 years is getting married and asks you to give a special toast or speech at the wedding reception in front of 200 guests.

    a.   I am scared about having to write the toast and give the speech in front of 200 people.

    b.   I am going to ruin this toast, say the wrong words, and disappoint my friend.

    c.   I will research wedding toasts and personalize a great toast for my friend's wedding.

    d.   I am very excited to do this for my friend because I know that my toast will be very special and my friend will appreciate my efforts.

8. Your boss tells you that you are going to get a considerable raise if you agree to write a one page monthly newsletter that will be distributed to all employees and customers.

   a. I am distressed because I am not a writer or editor.

   b. I know that I can't do this. I will tell my boss to get someone else who is more experienced with writing to do the newsletter.

   c. I am going to start researching newsletters from other companies to get creative ideas and reach out to writers on my team who are willing to submit articles.

   d. I will produce a phenomenal newsletter that will be a positive reflection upon my company.

9. The CEO or president of the company you work for approaches you and gives you a million dollar check and tells you to find charitable organizations that are honest. You are entrusted with donating the money to the charities and reporting back directly to the CEO or president.

   a. I am afraid that I won't be able to find honest charities. I am also terrified about being responsible for a million dollars.

   b. I know that I won't be able to find trustworthy charities and the CEO or president will be very disappointed.

   c. I start to investigate charitable organizations that are honest. I document the money that I give to each charity and provide a summary for the CEO or president.

   d. This is an exciting opportunity for me to help worthwhile charities. I will find great organizations that I can donate the money to.

10. You are asked to schedule an entire business trip for your boss and his wife. You are given his credit card and you have to make the reservations for the plane, hotel, limo, and restaurants. The boss tells you that he wants the best of everything.

    a.   I am scared that I won't live up to the expectations of my boss and he will be disappointed and upset.

    b.   I will make all the wrong choices and I ask my boss to find someone else to do this.

    c.   I tell my boss that I will handle everything. I will begin my research and find a highly respected airline, luxury hotel, a top rated limo company, and upscale restaurants.

    d.   I am confident that I will book a phenomenal business trip for my boss and his wife and they will be very happy.

11. You have to make dinner reservations at an exclusive restaurant for the president of the company. This is a very important business meeting with top clients who invest millions of dollars every year. You are asked to choose the entire menu with two different entrees and all of the side dishes.

    a.   I am very anxious about choosing the appropriate menu and I am worried that the president will be disappointed with my choices.

    b.   I can't do this because I will make all the wrong choices.

    c.   I decide to call the restaurant and ask them in detail about available options. I also ask them which menu items are the most popular.

    d.   I am excited for this opportunity because I know that the president and clients will enjoy my menu selections.

12. You are taking a class at your local college and the instructor calls you on your cell phone and tells you that he can't make it

to class today. He asks you to make an announcement to your classmates that the class in canceled. He also wants you to give the homework assignment for the next week.

a.   I am very apprehensive about speaking in front of the class.

b.   I am sure that I will give the wrong information to my classmates. I ask my instructor to get someone else to do this.

c.   I will prepare my thoughts ahead of time, advise my classmates that the instructor can't make it to class today, and give them the homework assignment for next week.

d.   I know that my classmates will be happy that I shared the information with them.

13. You are involved in a club related to a hobby that you love. The president of the club personally asks you to become his vice president. He tells you that he will explain all required duties to you in detail.

a.   I have never done anything like this before and I am nervous about this responsibility.

b.   I will make a lot of mistakes that will affect the club in a negative manner.

c.   I embrace this challenge and I will do my research to ensure that I know how to perform all the tasks for this position.

d.   I am confident that I will be a great vice president and I will help the club in a positive manner.

14. Your boss comes to you and tells you that he has to give a five minute presentation at a seminar. He gives you his speech and asks you to prepare a PowerPoint or Keynote Presentation for him. He also provides you with templates you can use.

a. I am very intimidated by this assignment and worried that the boss will be disappointed in my presentation that I prepare for him.

b. The presentation will look terrible and I know that my boss will be upset with me.

c. I may have limited knowledge or no experience with Power Point or Keynote but I am willing to do my research to ensure that the presentation looks professional.

d. The presentation is only five minutes, the boss is giving me templates, and the internet has a lot of helpful videos on both PowerPoint and Keynote. My presentation will look great and my boss will be happy.

15. You give $250,000 to your financial adviser. He wants to put your entire amount into an unstable investment and there is a high probability that you will lose it all. He will not back down and tells you that if you don't like his choice, you can take your money back and invest it yourself.

a. I have never invested this amount of money before and I am really scared to do it on my own.

b. If I invest the $250,000, I know that I will end up making the wrong decisions and will lose my money.

c. I decide to invest the money on my own. This is a definite challenge but I will commit to doing research so that I can make a wise choice with my investment.

d. I tell the financial adviser that I want my money back. I am confident that I will choose an investment that will be safe and generate a substantial increase.

16. Your best friend of twenty years is opening a nationally recognized submarine sandwich restaurant and she asks you to

pick the best location for her store. She wants an area with the highest amount of vehicular and foot traffic possible that will generate a lot of customers.

a. I am very nervous at the thought of even attempting to do something like this for my best friend.

b. I know that I am going to pick a terrible location that won't generate any business for my friend's submarine sandwich restaurant.

c. I am happy to help my friend and I begin searching for a number of locations that could be a possibility. Then, I will visit them in person to ensure that they have high traffic.

d. Even though I may never have done this in the past, I am positive that I will find an excellent location for my best friend's restaurant.

17. A close family member is achieving their dream of having their own business. They come to you and personally ask you to find a graphic designer that can create a highly professional logo for their brand new business. They tell you that money is no object and they trust your opinion.

a. I am very worried about finding a graphic designer who will do a great job on the logo.

b. I know that the final logo is going to look terrible and my family member will be upset with me.

c. I am going to start researching graphic designers and evaluating their past work on other logos until I find one that does a remarkable job for my family member.

d. The graphic designer that I choose is going to design the best possible logo for my family member.

18. The president of the corporation you work for asks you to reach out to the number one motivational speaker within the industry. He wants you to get this speaker for an hour keynote speech at an upcoming seminar. The corporation has a lot of money and they will pay whatever the fee is but you have to contact this person and arrange everything.

    a. I have never done anything like this before and I am frightened because I have to deal with the number one motivational speaker in the industry.

    b. There is no way that I would ever get this speaker for my company's upcoming seminar… Why even try?

    c. This sounds like a fun challenge. It will take some work but I am willing to give it a try and make it happen.

    d. I am confident knowing that I will make contact with the speaker and he will do the seminar.

19. The president of the company you work for wants to promote you to department head and give you a substantial raise in salary. With this position, you will be responsible for the following: hiring, training, disciplinary action, and firing of employees.

    a. I am terrified to have this type of responsibility. I have never done anything like this before and I am worried.

    b. I know that I am going to do poorly in this position and I will have to refuse the offer.

    c. This is a definite challenge but I am willing to talk to other department heads and learn their tips and strategies.

    d. I know that I am going to make a great department head. The employees and president of the company will be very happy with me in this position.

Millionaire Legacy™ Mindset Assessment | 215

20. The owner of the company you work for wants to launch a brand new product and tells you to pick the best advertising method: television, radio, newspaper, or billboard advertising. You can only use one medium to promote the launch. The owner asks you to pick the one that will generate the best results.

    a. I am apprehensive about choosing the best advertising method.

    b. I am going to choose the wrong advertising medium and the launch will turn out badly.

    c. I am excited about this opportunity to promote a brand new product into the marketplace and I start researching all of the advertising methods in order to pick the one that will generate the best return on investment.

    d. I am confident that whatever medium I choose will generate tremendous results and the owner will be very satisfied with me.

21. Your sales manager calls you and tells you that he is quitting immediately. He scheduled a dinner with a high profile individual who is interested in becoming a client of your company. You will have to attend this meeting and convince this respected individual to become one of your clients. This is the only time that he can meet with you and this deal could be worth millions of dollars in revenue.

    a. I begin to panic because I am not prepared to handle such an important meeting.

    b. I know that I am going to make huge mistakes and the high profile individual will not become my client.

    c. This is definitely a challenge but I quickly write down an outline of key elements that I will share with the potential client.

    d.   I can definitely help this individual and I will convey this message to him in an effective manner. As a result, he will become a client.

22. You get a phone call from your accountant who tells you that he got a higher paying job and he is leaving immediately. He is an authorized signer on your business accounts and is the only person at your company who knows all of your finances, passwords, and access codes. He hangs up the phone and he won't take your calls.

    a.   I am worried that he could take all the money from my accounts.

    b.   I have no idea what I am going to do now and this could be the end of my business.

    c.   This presents a real challenge but I will begin by calling my bank and immediately removing all of his access to my accounts. Then, I will decide what person will be responsible for handling the accounting duties.

    d.   There are a number of things to be done but I am confident that I will find a trusted person to be my new accountant.

23. You conduct your own seminar and give a great talk. At the end of your speech, you give a presentation on your products and you ask the people at your event to make a purchase. You are excited but no one at the event decides to make any purchase from you.

    a.   I start to panic because I know that my business will not be able to survive without any clients.

    b.   I knew that I wouldn't make any sales. I might have to close my business.

c. This was a definite wake-up call. I begin to evaluate what I did wrong and study other presenters to determine how to correctly position my offer so that people will buy from me at future events.

d. I know that, after more research, I will be able to pick the best methods to encourage people to buy from me in the future. As a result, I will make a lot of sales.

24. Your uncle is willing to give you his small business which is a nationally recognized franchise. You worked part time for your uncle for several years and you enjoyed it. The business has established clientele and makes a substantial profit every month.

a. I am terrified at the thought of running the business and will have to reject my uncle's offer.

b. Even though this is a nationally recognized franchise and my uncle makes a profit every month, I know that I will lose money and won't be able to pay the bills.

c. This is a challenge but I am willing to do my homework in order to ensure that it works out very well.

d. This is a great opportunity and I know that I will continue to make a profit. My uncle will be very happy with my results.

25. You are contacted by a highly respected university. They are willing to pay you $15,000 for an hour keynote talk on your area of expertise. Your speech will be in front of students, faculty members, and parents.

a. I am scared about having to give a keynote speech in front of a large audience.

b. I will do poorly with this speech and it won't sound good.

c.   This opportunity is exciting and I will start working on my Power Point or Keynote presentation so that I can include all of my key points that I want to share with the audience.

d.   I will give a great speech and everyone in attendance will gain a lot of information from me.

Millionaire Legacy™ Mindset Assessment
Scoring Chart

Enter your response to each question by filling in the circles below. After you complete the assessment, add up the number of highlighted circles in each column for (a), (b), (c), and (d).

Question	(a)	(b)	(c)	(d)	Question
1	O	O	O	O	1
2	O	O	O	O	2
3	O	O	O	O	3
4	O	O	O	O	4
5	O	O	O	O	5
6	O	O	O	O	6
7	O	O	O	O	7
8	O	O	O	O	8
9	O	O	O	O	9
10	O	O	O	O	10
11	O	O	O	O	11
12	O	O	O	O	12
13	O	O	O	O	13
14	O	O	O	O	14
15	O	O	O	O	15
16	O	O	O	O	16
17	O	O	O	O	17
18	O	O	O	O	18
19	O	O	O	O	19
20	O	O	O	O	20
21	O	O	O	O	21
22	O	O	O	O	22
23	O	O	O	O	23
24	O	O	O	O	24
25	O	O	O	O	25
Column Totals					

Calculate your score:

Count the total number of each answer in the above columns and enter that number on the corresponding lines listed below. Then, multiply that number by 4 to obtain your percentage.

Total number of A's highlighted = _____ times (x) 4 = _____ %

Total number of B's highlighted = _____ times (x) 4 = _____ %

Total number of C's highlighted = _____ times (x) 4 = _____ %

Total number of D's highlighted = _____ times (x) 4 = _____ %

Take the above percentages and transfer them to the Millionaire Legacy™ Mindset Assessment Report.

Millionaire Legacy™ Mindset Assessment Report
Transfer your scores into the "My Score" areas.

(A)	(B)	(C)	(D)
Fear	Failure	Perseverance	Success
My Score: _____%	My Score: _____%	My Score: _____%	My Score: _____%
Millionaires score very low in these two areas.		Millionaires score very high in these two areas.	
A high score within the (A) column indicates that your mindset is focused on fear. When you are presented with situations that scare you, you have a tendency to back away and avoid them.		A high score within the (C) column indicates that your mindset is focused on having perseverance. When you are presented with challenging tasks, you will discover innovative ways to solve the problem.	
A high score within the (B) column indicates that your mindset is focused on failure. When you are presented with challenging events, your inclination is to focus on failing at the task.		A high score within the (D) column indicates that your mindset is focused on success. When you encounter obstacles, you will find creative ways in order to become successful.	

*Your use of the Millionaire Legacy™ Mindset Assessment, Report, and Evaluation of Results constitutes your agreement to the provisions of the disclaimer.

MILLIONAIRE LEGACY™ MINDSET ASSESSMENT

EVALUATION OF RESULTS

Fear and Failure

If you received your highest percentage from column (a), this indicates that you are focused on being fearful. As a result, you may want to turn and run away from any situation which is causing you fear. With this type of mindset, you may become nervous to the point where you feel emotionally paralyzed and unable to make any advancement forward.

If you received your highest percentage from column (b), this indicates that you are focused on failure. When an obstacle is thrown into your path, you will find all the reasons why you are going to fail. With this type of mindset, you may have low self-esteem and a negative self-image of yourself.

Millionaire Mindset Action Steps for Fear and Failure

If you scored high within the fear or failure columns, these are two areas that must be changed in a positive direction. View this as an educational learning experience, admit your challenges, and be willing to change your perception regarding both of these issues. After you are able to accomplish this, you will ensure that your mindset is similar to that of a millionaire.

Action steps to overcome fear and failure:

1. Minimize and eliminate your fears.
2. Replace any thought of failure with a strong confidence of being successful.
3. Recognize that fear and failure are only temporary.

4. Remain focused on your final objective.
5. Understand that you have the power and control to reshape your thinking from a negative perspective to a positive one.

Perseverance and Success

If you received your highest percentage from column (c), this indicates that you are focused on perseverance. When you encounter a challenge, you become creative and openly embrace this opportunity to find an innovative solution. With this type of mindset, you are a determined and self-assured individual.

If you received your highest percentage from column (d), this indicates that you are focused on success. Whatever setback or hardship is thrown into your path, you are confident that you will be successful. With this type of mindset, you exhibit high self-esteem, self-confidence, and have a very positive outlook on life.

Millionaire Mindset Action Steps for Perseverance and Success

If you scored high within the perseverance or success columns, these are two areas that can be enhanced even further. With this type of mindset, you are closely aligned with the same type of mental thought process which is utilized by millionaires to achieve phenomenal success.

Action steps to enhance perseverance and success:

1. Continue to develop innovative solutions for any challenges which are encountered.
2. Remain vigilant and prepared for any unexpected event.
3. Strengthen your commitment to push through any setbacks.
4. Disregard any negative thoughts and maintain your focus on a successful outcome.

5. Pursue your dreams, goals, and aspirations being confident that you will achieve them.

The Millionaire Legacy™ Mindset Assessment, Scoring Chart, Assessment Report, and Evaluation of Results may NOT be copied, published, or duplicated in any manner without the consent of the author. Copies of this assessment may be purchased for your company, organization, or school upon request from the author. Please visit MillionaireLegacy.com.

8 Millionaire Success Strategies Mind Maps

Millionaire Strategy #1 Mind Map
Develop a Business Plan and Clearly Defined Personal Goals

#1 - Calculate expenses, revenue, profits, and list the steps to achieve your personal goals

Estimate Projected Expenses
- Look at Estimated Revenue
- Anticipate possible profits
Analyze cost of customer acquisition

#2 - Generate a strategy for acquiring customers and keeping them

Collect emails from potential customers and clients
Offer a customer something of value in return for email
- Offer higher discounts for your customers
- Utilize concept of reciprocity

#3 - Develop your business plan and begin a dream board

Determine what steps are needed to achieve your business goals
- Make a list of required steps that need to be taken
- Welcome suggestions from your employees
- Make a list of your personal goals
- Use a Dream Board

© Millionaire Legacy™

Millionaire Strategy #2 Mind Map
Overcoming Fear

Will be presented with roadblocks
Fear rises to conscious level
Don't focus on fear
Minimize your mental perception of what is making you fearful

#1 - Don't Focus on Fear; Minimize It

Visualize your eventual goal
Embrace your fear
Use persistence to push through fear
Refocus your mindset
Become clearly focused on what you want

#2 - Visualize the Bigger Picture; Your Goal

Have a clear plan
Write your plan down in a concise manner
Conquer any doubt; Disregard any uncertainty
Focus your attention on High-Priority Tasks
Take Action Steps every day toward reaching your goals and dreams

#3 - Decide on a Plan and Take Action

Millionaire Strategy #3 Mind Map
Failure is an Option

#1 - Turn Failure into an Educational Experience

Use your failure as a learning process
Don't take it personally
Gain insight from your failure
Develop an effective solution

#2 - Clear Your Mind, take a break and look again with a refreshed perspective

Get away from your office or home
Remove yourself from the situation, clear your mind
Develop a refreshed perspective and perfect solution
Allow your mind to become clearly focused
Write down or record your ideas

#3 - Create a New Solution

"Temporary defeat is Not permanent failure" ...Napolean Hill
Become flexible and open to possible solutions
Brainstorm with your team members
Embrace the strategies that work
Try the new solution to determine effectiveness

© Millionaire Legacy™

Millionaire Strategy #4 Mind Map
Importance of Having a Mentor or Coach

#1 - Find a Mentor or Coach

Do your homework and research

Seek out experts within your specific area

Invest in expert's books, home study courses, seminars, etc.

Begin your journey in steps and work your way up to respected expert

Select a mentor with a proven track record of generating substantial and tangible results

#2 - Become a member of a Master Mind Group

Receive guidance and support from a Master Mind Group

Brainstorm with other members to devise effective strategies

Great support system to help you reach your goals and dreams

Members share tips, strategies, and techniques with each other

Be inspired to your highest level of excellence

#3 - Invest in Continuing Education with Home Study Courses, Seminars and Books

Home Study Courses, Seminars, and Books are very helpful

Home Study Courses: advance through them at your own pace

Seminars: meet experts and learn their secrets directly

Books: important role in the mentoring process

Continuing Education is critical to your ongoing success

Millionaire Strategy #5 Mind Map
Having Persistence and Pushing Forward

Center your attention on pursuing your highest ambition

#1 - Pursue your highest ambition; clarify what you want to achieve

Get refocused on what you really want both professionally and personally

Live life vibrantly and energetically

Keep growing and expanding; don't sit back and let life pass you by

Promise to yourself that you will not give up and walk away

#2 - Don't Give Up, Don't Walk Away

Perseverance is critical for your eventual success

You are rewarded for taking action; if you don't do anything, then you will not get anything back in return

Give 100% to reaching what you want from life

Visualize your dreams as if you are living them now; post images of your goals on a dream board

Hold yourself accountable by scheduling your projects on a calendar

#3 - Schedule your projects on a calendar; promise a completion date

By writing things down on a calendar, it is more difficult to push things off

With a deadline and predetermined date of completion, this will give you motivation to accomplish your tasks

Brush off any challenges and setbacks

Completion date on a calendar is motivating force for finishing the project

© Millionaire Legacy™

Millionaire Strategy #6 Mind Map
Mindset for Success

Millionaires love life

Maintain a positive attitude that transmits energy and enthusiasm

Live your passion and do what you love on a daily basis

Look inside your heart and soul to discover your passion

Have a genuine concern for helping others and not with getting rich.... then, wealth will flow automatically to you

#1 - Celebrate life with energy and enthusiasm; live your passion

See yourself in possession of the amount of money you desire

According to Bob Proctor, you need a mindset for productivity and growth

Replace the poverty way of thinking with thoughts of prosperity

According to James Malinchak:
1. Develop the right mindset
2. Get the appropriate skillset
3. Take the required action

Wealth allows you to expand, grow, and help others

#2 - Develop a prosperity consciousness

Natural desire to grow, expand, and learn on this life journey

Become active with continuing education

Read books, invest in home study courses, attend seminars, seek out a mentor, and become involved with master mind groups

Set ambitions that you want to achieve

Growth continues in an upward direction regardless of age

#3 - Accelerate your intellectual growth toward a higher level

© Millionaire Legacy™

Millionaire Strategy #7 Mind Map
Generosity and Gratitude

When you give, it must be done with a "Pureness of Heart"

Don't expect anything back in return when you give

When you appreciate the concept of sharing and giving, you will be blessed emotionally and financially

Secret from inner circle of millionaires; give without any anticipation of receiving anything in return

Appreciate the blessings you currently have and be thankful for what you are going to receive in the future

#1 - Give with a pureness of heart and have gratitude

Do a small act of kindness for three people every week

By doing three small acts of kindness, an energetic vibrational wave will be sent out to the universe and you will receive it back

According to Mark Victor Hansen, "give ten, save ten, invest ten, and live on seventy percent of your income"

Engage in Tithing... give ten percent of your income to a church, charitable organization or to someone in financial need

"Giving guarantees receiving" ...Mark Victor Hansen

#2 - Perform "Three Small Acts of Kindness"

Create high quality products that solve a problem

Don't become focused on only making money

Share your knowledge with your customers and clients

Provide high quality goods and services

#3 - Create high quality products, services, and coaching programs

© Millionaire Legacy™

Millionaire Strategy #8 Mind Map
Taking Decisive Action: Magnetic Action Principle (MAP)

#1 - Develop an effective time management plan

By using effective time management skills, you can find time to work on what you want to achieve

Time is going to pass by at the same rate whether you are doing nothing or if you are actively taking steps toward reaching your dreams

Devote the time to work on projects that will bring you closer to your objectives

Spend a half hour in the morning and evening toward working on your goals

Listen to home study courses and audio courses when you are in the car or shopping

#2 - Research options and make decisions quickly

Do your homework and make an informed decision

Don't miss a great deal because of procrastination or hesitation

Sometimes, our best choices are made quickly and based upon our intuition

Get suggestions from a trusted adviser or business associate

Successful people make a decision in an efficient manner after they have been presented with all the facts

#3 - Take decisive action

Negative internal scripts or attitudes have to be discarded

Write down your goals and dreams and post it in a prominent location so that you can see them every day

Center your focus on completing high priority tasks related to your objectives

Don't make excuses for inactivity

Become focused on taking the necessary steps to obtain your goals

© Millionaire Legacy™

Key Elements for Employee Motivation
Mind Map

Key Elements for Employee Motivation
Mind Map

Ask your employees what motivates them

As noted by James Malinchak, department heads should determine what motivates everyone on their team

MONEY does not motivate everyone

Russell Brunson gives his staff a survey to determine what motivates them

Don't guess at what an employee wants; just ask them what they would like to have

 # 1 - Determine what motivates each of your employees individually

Let your employees know you appreciate the hard work they are doing for you

If you treat your team with respect, they will be more likely to go above and beyond their duties

Your staff can be challenged in a diplomatic manner

Here are the steps to resolve an area of concern with an employee:

1. Give your employee praise for the great job they are doing.
2. Explain their mistake or problematic behavior in a non-critical manner.
3. Provide support and give respect to your employee. Let them know they are a valued member of your business and you appreciate all of their dedication and hard work.

When an employee leaves your meeting feeling you value their contributions, they are more likely to change the problem behavior

 # 2 - Praise your employees for a great job, correct their mistakes in a non-critical manner, and thank them for their contributions to your company

Be willing and receptive to accept help from your employees

Create an environment where people enjoy working together

Steve Harrison welcomes suggestions. He told his employees to picture themselves running the company and asked the following questions:

1. What would you get rid of that we're doing now?
2. What would you add?
3. What would you do differently?
4. What do you think that people really want?
5. What do you wish we had?

Invite your team to give their suggestions and advice

 # 3 - Openly welcome suggestions from team members

REFERENCES

Burchard, B. (2011). *The millionaire messenger: Make a difference and a fortune sharing your advice.* New York: Free Press.

Clark, J., & Cooper, A. L. (2013). *Nothing stood in her way* (3rd ed.). Lexington, KY: CreateSpace Independent Publishing Platform.

Hill, N. (2007). *Think & grow rich.* Rockville, MD: ARC Manor.

Kleinman, P. (2012). *Psych 101: Psychology facts, basics, statistics, tests, and more!.* Avon, Mass: Adams Media.

Kozlowski, S. W. (2012). *The Oxford handbook of organizational psychology: Volume 1.* New York: Oxford University Press.

Lewin, K., Lippit, R. and White, R.K. (1939). Patterns of aggressive behavior in experimentally created social climates. *Journal of Social Psychology, 10,* 271-301

Maslow, A. H. (2013). *A theory of human motivation.* (Reprint of 1943 edition) Martino Fine Books. (Original Publication: Psychological review, Vol 50(4), Jul 1943, 370-396)

Maslow, A. H. (2004). *The Psychology of Science: A Reconnaissance.* Retrieved from http://www.abrahammaslow.com/books.html

Merton, R. K. (1968). *Social theory and social structure.* New York: Free Press.

Nevid, J. S. (2009). *Essentials of psychology: Concepts and applications.* Boston, MA: Houghton Mifflin.

Seligman, M. E. (2006). *Learned optimism: How to change your mind and your life.* New York: Vintage Books.

Sullenberger, C., & Zaslow, J. (2009). *Highest duty: My search for what really matters.* New York: William Morrow.

Tracy, B. (2000). *The 100 absolutely unbreakable laws of business success.* San Francisco: Berrett-Koehler.

Tracy, B. (2004). *The psychology of selling: How to sell more, easier, and faster than you ever thought possible.* Nashville: Thomas Nelson Publishers.

Weiten, W., & Lloyd, M. A. (2006). *Psychology applied to modern life: Adjustment in the 21st century.* California: Thomson/Wadsworth.

Ziglar, Z. (2012). *Inspiration from the top: [a collection of my favorite quotes].* Nashville: Thomas Nelson.

WEBSITES

ColonelSanders.com - Biography. (n.d.). Retrieved from
    http://colonelsanders.com/bio.asp

EAA | Experimental Aircraft Association | Oshkosh, Wisconsin. (n.d.).
    Retrieved from http://www.eaa.org

EAA Young Eagles. (n.d.). Retrieved from http://www.youngeagles.org

Julie Clark Airshows. (n.d.). Retrieved from
    http://julieclarkairshows.com

Karolyn Grimes who played Zuzu in "It's A Wonderful Life". (n.d.).
    Retrieved from http://www.zuzu.net

Sean D. Tucker | Team Oracle. (n.d.). Retrieved from
    https://www.oracle.com/corporate/teamoracle/sean-tucker.html

St. Jude Children's Research Hospital. (n.d.). Retrieved from
    http://www.stjude.org

Sully Sullenberger (n.d.). Retrieved from http://sullysullenberger.com

2011 - 05/25 - You Are Never Too Old to Earn Your College Degree.
    (n.d.). Retrieved from http://spirit.eaa.org/apps/obituaries/
    MemorialWall2.aspx?ID=2503

MILLIONAIRE LEGACY INDEX

To receive a Complimentary Copy of the

"4 Critical Elements to Achieving Success,"

Please visit:

www.MillionaireLegacy.com

We will email you a copy in PDF format that can be printed out and placed in a prominent location where it can be seen on a daily basis.

Printed in the USA
CPSIA information can be obtained
at www.ICGtesting.com
JSHW022216140824
68134JS00018B/1082